# Back to the Start Button

## Tracing the PlayStation Era's Timeless Legacy

By Fabrizio Vassallo

**Disclaimer**

All trademarks, service marks, trade names, trade dress, product names, and logos appearing in this book are the property of their respective owners. Any reference to them does not imply any affiliation with or endorsement by them. All content, stories, and information presented in this book are based on the author's research, experiences, and personal opinions. While every effort has been made to ensure the accuracy and reliability of the information provided, the author and publisher make no warranties, express or implied, and shall not be held responsible or liable for any errors, omissions, or inaccuracies in the information or for any user's reliance on this information.

This book is meant for informational and entertainment purposes only and is not intended as a replacement or substitute for any professional advice, financial, medical, or otherwise.

---

# Introduction: Before the Boom

## The World Before PlayStation – Arcade Salons, Bedroom Coders, and Chunky Cartridges

The 1990s. For many, it was an era defined by baggy jeans, MTV, and the dawn of the World Wide Web. But for gamers, it was a period of anticipation, a time when gaming's finest hour was just over the horizon. The journey, however, didn't start with the high-pitched chime of a PlayStation booting up. No, dear reader, it began in dimly lit arcades, cluttered bedrooms with whirring computers, and the unmistakable clunk of a cartridge slotting into place.

Remember arcades? Before malls were dotted with hipster cafes and escape rooms, they boasted of vast, cavernous spaces known as "arcade salons." Buzzing neon lights beckoned players inside, where a cacophony of bleeps, bloops, and synthesized music created a symphony of electronic chaos. The air was a heady mix of popcorn, cheap cologne, and adolescent ambition. Players, armed with a pocketful of coins, would challenge one another for the top spot on the scoreboard. It wasn't just about playing; it was a social gathering spot. You didn't just go to the arcade to play; you went to **be seen** playing.

In contrast to the public allure of arcades, the bedroom coders painted a different picture. These were the unsung heroes of the gaming world, working from their personal sanctuaries (or, you know, cluttered bedrooms). With the rise of home computers like the Commodore 64 and ZX Spectrum, creating games became a possibility for the common man. Armed with a mix of coding knowledge, unbridled passion, and a gallon of caffeinated drinks, these individuals crafted games that, while often lacking the polish of bigger titles, had heart. And bugs. Oh, so many bugs. But that was part of the charm!

And then, there were the cartridges. Chunky, durable, and often infuriating, these were the preferred medium for console games. Forget the loading times of CDs; if a game on a cartridge didn't boot, it was ritual time. Gamers became experts in the "blow on the cartridge" technique, a mystic ritual passed down from elder sibling to younger. Some claim it was purely psychological, while others swear by its efficacy. One thing was certain – everyone had their own "special technique."

The world before PlayStation was a simpler time, yet it was rich with experiences that laid the groundwork for the gaming revolution that was about to come. The stage was set, and the players (pun absolutely intended) were eager for the next level.

# The Rise of the 'Gamer' Stereotype and the Seeds of Change

As the arcade culture flourished and bedroom coding grew in popularity, a new identity began to emerge from the flickering screens and tangles of joystick wires: the 'gamer.' But who was this mythical creature? In the eyes of mainstream media and the popular kids at school, they were often basement-dwellers, bathed in the glow of their screens, socially awkward, and with an uncanny ability to recite cheat codes like their life depended on it. The term 'gamer' wasn't just an identifier; it became a stereotype, a label slapped onto anyone who seemed too engrossed in their pixelated worlds.

But was that all there was to the story? Of course not! Gamers were a diverse bunch. From the cool dude at the arcade effortlessly setting the high score in 'Street Fighter' to the school nerd who'd just discovered the joys of 'Dungeons & Dragons,' gamers came from all walks of life. Yes, there were the introverts who preferred the company of their in-game companions, but there were also extroverts who thrived in multiplayer environments, turning gaming sessions into raucous social events.

Yet, the seeds of change were sprouting. With gaming becoming more accessible and widespread, the line between "gamer" and "non-gamer" began to blur. Parents, who once dismissed games as mindless entertainment, were now teaming up with their kids for a round of 'Mario Kart.' Even celebrities, the gods of popular culture, admitted to indulging in a bit of button-mashing now and then.

Gaming magazines, once relegated to the back shelves, started to find their way onto coffee tables and in school backpacks. Television shows and news segments began to feature gaming competitions. Suddenly, it was becoming cool to be a gamer. But with this newfound acceptance came its own set of challenges. The gaming community, once a tight-knit group, now found itself grappling with issues of inclusivity, representation, and the very definition of what it meant to be a "gamer."

The gaming landscape was shifting. As the 90s marched on, those seeds of change would grow into something bigger, heralding the dawn of a new era. An era where gaming would step out from the shadows and proudly claim its place in mainstream culture.

# Chapter 1: Sony's Wild Card

## Introduction to Sony's Gamble in the Gaming Market

The early 90s were a strange time in the world of electronics. Companies known for manufacturing televisions, radios, and VCRs were vying for a slice of the lucrative gaming market pie. Many industry pundits saw gaming as a fad, something that would fade away just like pet rocks or disco. But then, along came a major player from an unexpected corner: Sony.

Sony was no stranger to risk. Having established itself as a giant in the entertainment and electronics industry, the company had a reputation for innovation. The Walkman, after all, had revolutionized the way we listened to music. But venturing into gaming? That was uncharted territory.

It all began rather innocuously. In the late 80s, Sony entered into a collaboration with Nintendo to create a CD-ROM add-on for the Super Nintendo Entertainment System (SNES). The idea was simple: combine Sony's prowess in audio-visual tech with Nintendo's gaming might. The project was affectionately named the "Play Station," a hybrid console that would play both cartridges and CDs.

However, like many high-profile collaborations, it was fraught with disagreements. Differences in vision, disputes over licensing, and a myriad of other issues led to a public falling out between the two giants at the 1991 Consumer Electronics Show. It was a blow to Sony's pride, a very public humiliation. But as the saying goes, "When one door closes, another opens." Instead of retreating, Sony decided to double down.

Sony's leadership, particularly Ken Kutaragi, often dubbed the "Father of the PlayStation," believed in the potential of a CD-based gaming system. They envisioned a console that wasn't just about games but an entertainment hub. But this wasn't a simple endeavor. Sony was a newcomer, attempting to carve a niche in a market dominated by veterans like Sega and Nintendo.

Many within Sony were skeptical. The gaming world was seen as a children's playground, a stark contrast to Sony's brand which was associated with high-end, sophisticated electronics. But Kutaragi and his team persisted. They believed that gaming was evolving, that it wasn't just kids who were playing, but adults too. And where there was a diverse audience, there was an opportunity.

As development began in earnest, Sony sought feedback from game developers, a step that was both smart and crucial. Game developers had long felt constrained by the limited storage capacity of cartridges. CDs, with their larger storage space, presented a world of possibilities: richer graphics, full-motion video, and CD-quality audio. Developers were enthralled. Games could now be more cinematic, more immersive.

Yet, the road to the PlayStation's creation was filled with challenges. The first prototype units were bulky, the operating system was unstable, and developers, though excited, were also wary. They needed assurance that Sony was in this for the long haul, not just as a passing fancy. After all, the gaming graveyard was filled with consoles that promised much but delivered little.

But Sony was playing for keeps. They invested heavily in marketing, forging alliances with major game developers, and ensuring that the PlayStation had a diverse game library at launch. More importantly, they pitched the PlayStation not just as a gaming console, but as a lifestyle product. Their target audience was broader – it wasn't just the teenage gamer, but also the college student, the young adult, the parent who had grown up on a steady diet of Atari and arcade games.

By the time the PlayStation was unveiled to the public in December 1994, the buzz was palpable. But it was also accompanied by whispers of doubt. Could Sony, a newcomer, really break into a market ruled by gaming behemoths? Was the world ready for a shift from cartridges to CDs?

The PlayStation's release was not just the launch of a new console, but a statement of intent. Sony was signaling its entry into a new realm, ready to reshape the contours of the gaming world. They were not just playing the game; they were aiming to redefine it.

But as any gamer knows, starting a game is one thing; it's how you play that determines the outcome. And the PlayStation's journey had only just begun.

# The Unexpected Success and Genesis of the PlayStation

With the PlayStation's inception, Sony had thrown its hat into an arena where many had perished. Pundits and gamers, loyal to their respective consoles, looked on with a mix of curiosity and skepticism. While Sony had a formidable reputation in the electronics world, gaming was a different beast. It wasn't just about fancy hardware; it was about capturing the hearts and imaginations of its audience.

## 1. The Birth Pains

In its early days, Sony faced a plethora of challenges. For starters, the gaming community had its doubts. Could a CD-based system truly offer a gaming experience as rich, if not richer, than cartridge-based ones? Cartridges, for all their limitations, had near-instant load times. CDs, on the other hand, had an irritating tendency to lag.

There were also the economic challenges. The R&D for the PlayStation was expensive, and with each prototype, costs mounted. The initial price point Sony had in mind was considered high, a potential deterrent for families and casual gamers.

Then there were internal disagreements. Not everyone within Sony was on board. Some believed the company was overreaching, stepping into a territory best left to the likes of Nintendo and Sega.

But as development progressed, it became clear that the PlayStation wasn't just another console; it was a technological marvel. Its graphics, sound quality, and gameplay capabilities were beginning to surpass expectations. Developers, initially wary, were now looking at the PlayStation with renewed interest.

## 2. Building Alliances

Sony knew that to make the PlayStation a success, they needed games—good ones. They aggressively courted third-party developers, offering them favorable terms and a more open platform. Compared to Nintendo's notoriously strict licensing regime, Sony was a breath of fresh air.

Big names like Konami, Namco, and Square, who had previously aligned with Nintendo, were now releasing titles for the PlayStation. One of the major coups was the release of "Final Fantasy VII" by Square, a title originally intended for the Nintendo 64. With its cinematic graphics, compelling storyline, and unforgettable characters, FFVII became a flagship title, showcasing the PlayStation's capabilities.

## 3. Marketing Mastery

Sony's marketing for the PlayStation was nothing short of revolutionary. Instead of just targeting children, they aimed at a wider demographic: teenagers, college students, and even young adults. Their ads were edgy, stylish, and sometimes downright bizarre, reflecting the eclectic nature of the 90s.

Their message was clear: The PlayStation was not just a toy; it was an entertainment system, a status symbol, a must-have gadget for the discerning individual.

## 4. Launch and Reception

On December 3, 1994, the PlayStation was released in Japan. Within hours, it was clear that Sony had a hit on their hands. Stores sold out, and there were reports of long lines, reminiscent of the frenzy usually reserved for blockbuster movie releases or new music albums.

When the PlayStation hit the North American and European markets in 1995, the reception was equally enthusiastic. While it faced stiff competition from Sega's Saturn and the impending launch of Nintendo's N64, the PlayStation had an ace up its sleeve – its games. Titles like "Tekken," "Resident Evil," and "Ridge Racer" showcased the console's versatility, catering to different genres and tastes.

By the end of 1996, just two years after its release, the PlayStation had sold over 10 million units worldwide. It wasn't just the sales figures that were impressive; it was the cultural impact. The PlayStation was becoming synonymous with gaming, with many using the term "PlayStation" interchangeably with "gaming console."

## 5. Setting the Standard

Sony's PlayStation did more than just offer a new way to play games; it set a new industry standard. The DualShock controller, introduced in 1997, became the blueprint for subsequent controllers, with its ergonomic design and dual analog sticks.

The PlayStation also popularized memory cards, allowing players to save their game progress.

## 6. The Challenges of Success

Yet, success brought its own set of challenges. As the PlayStation's popularity soared, so did the demand for new and better games. The competition wasn't standing still either. Nintendo's N64, with its iconic titles like "Super Mario 64" and "The Legend of Zelda: Ocarina of Time," was giving Sony a run for its money.

Piracy, too, emerged as a major concern. The very thing that made the PlayStation popular, its CD format, also made it vulnerable to piracy. Bootleg copies of games began flooding the market, leading to significant revenue losses.

However, despite these challenges, Sony's PlayStation had achieved what few thought possible. It had entered a market dominated by established players and not only carved a niche for itself but had reshaped the landscape altogether.

## 7. Genesis of a Legacy

By the time the 2000s rolled around, the PlayStation's impact was undeniable. It had opened the doors to a new era of gaming, one where visuals, sound, and storytelling took center stage. More importantly, it had expanded the gaming community, making it more inclusive and diverse.

The PlayStation's legacy wasn't just in its sales figures or its games. It lay in the memories it created, the friendships it forged, and the boundaries it pushed. Sony's gamble had paid off, and the gaming world would never be the same again.

# Sony's Rivals: A Look at Nintendo, Sega, and the Forgotten Ones

Amidst the buzz of the PlayStation, a theater of war was setting up in the gaming world. While Sony was the new kid on the block, there were seasoned warriors who had been battling it out for years. These titans – Nintendo and Sega – along with some lesser-known contenders, made the 90s a golden age of console warfare.

## 1. Nintendo: The Timeless Titan

No discussion about gaming in the 90s can commence without mentioning Nintendo. The Japanese giant had virtually defined home gaming in the 80s with its Nintendo Entertainment System (NES) and continued its domination with the Super Nintendo Entertainment System (SNES) in the early 90s.

**Legacy of the SNES:** The SNES, with its rich graphics and iconic titles like "Super Mario World" and "The Legend of Zelda: A Link to the Past," had set a high bar. The SNES emphasized quality over quantity, with a focus on captivating storytelling and innovative gameplay. Their partnership approach with game developers was, however, quite strict, often leading to disputes.

**The N64 Gambit**: In 1996, Nintendo launched the N64. With its 64-bit processor, it promised and often delivered unparalleled graphics and gameplay. Titles like "Super Mario 64" revolutionized 3D gaming, while "GoldenEye 007" set standards for multiplayer shooters. However, the N64 stuck with cartridges, which though faster, were more expensive and had less storage than CDs.

**Hesitation with Change:** Nintendo's cautious approach to technology often put it at odds with trends. Its reluctance to adopt CDs, for instance, had cost them their collaboration with Sony, leading to the birth of the PlayStation.

## 2. Sega: The Edgy Challenger

Sega had always been Nintendo's fiercest rival. Its marketing was aggressive, directly targeting Nintendo with the famous "Genesis does what Nintendon't" campaign.

**The Genesis/Mega Drive Era**: In the early 90s, the Sega Genesis (known as Mega Drive outside North America) was Nintendo's primary competitor. With a 16-bit processor and titles like "Sonic the Hedgehog," it appealed to an older audience, positioning itself as the cooler, edgier console.

**The Saturn Misstep**: Released in 1995, the Sega Saturn was a technical marvel, but it had its flaws. It was challenging to develop for, and its rushed release, intended to get a head start over the PlayStation, backfired. A lack of strong titles at launch and its high price made it lag behind both the PlayStation and the N64.

**Dreaming of Redemption**: Sega's last bid in the console market was the Dreamcast in 1999. Advanced and ahead of its time with features like online gaming, it had potential. But with Sony's PlayStation 2 on the horizon, it struggled to gain a foothold.

## 3. The Forgotten Ones

While Nintendo and Sega were the main players, the 90s saw several other companies try their luck in the console market, with varying degrees of success.

**Neo Geo:** SNK's Neo Geo was a powerhouse, offering arcade-quality games at home. However, its exorbitant cost made it a niche product. It found more success in arcades with its Multi Video System.

**3DO:** The brainchild of Electronic Arts founder Trip Hawkins, the 3DO was a CD-based system launched in 1993. Technologically advanced, it was hampered by its high price and lack of compelling exclusive games. It's often remembered for its quirky titles and innovative ideas.

**Atari Jaguar:** Atari, once the king of home gaming, made its final console bid with the Jaguar in 1993. Touted as the first 64-bit console, its complicated hardware and lack of developer support led to its downfall. Despite having a few memorable titles, it couldn't compete with the big players.

**TurboGrafx-16/PC Engine**: Released by NEC, the TurboGrafx-16 had considerable success in Japan as the PC

Engine but struggled in the North American market. Its CD add-on was one of the first of its kind, but a lack of marketing and standout titles hindered its potential.

## 4. The Landscape of Rivalry

The 90s console wars were more than just about hardware specs; they were about identities. Each console had its ethos, its personality. Nintendo was the family-friendly giant with a focus on timeless classics. Sega was the rebellious teenager, always looking to push boundaries. Sony, the newcomer, was the sophisticated young adult, blending cutting-edge technology with style.

This era was also a testament to the importance of games. Hardware drew people in, but it was the games that made them stay. Exclusives became crucial, as did partnerships with third-party developers.

## 5. Impact on the Industry

The fierce competition of the 90s led to rapid innovations. From graphics and gameplay to storytelling and music, each company pushed the other to do better. This decade laid the groundwork for the gaming industry's future, shaping it into the multi-billion-dollar behemoth it is today.

Moreover, the console wars also shaped cultures. From playground debates over which console was better to midnight launch events, being a "gamer" became a significant part of many people's identities.

# Chapter 2: Disc Over Cartridge – Why It Mattered

## The Dawn of the CD Era in Gaming

The gaming world is no stranger to evolutions, from pixelated Pong balls bouncing back and forth to sprawling, open-world adventures that blur the line between game and cinema. Yet, few transformations were as pivotal as the shift from cartridges to compact discs (CDs). Let's delve into why this mattered and how it shaped an era.

### 1. Storage: A Quantum Leap

Arguably the most significant advantage of CDs was their storage capacity. While cartridges were limited to a few megabytes, a CD could store hundreds. This vast difference opened the doors to:

- **More Comprehensive Games**: Longer narratives, intricate gameplay mechanics, and broader in-game universes became possible.

- **Enhanced Audio and Visuals**: CD-quality soundtracks replaced the chiptunes of yore, and full-motion video (FMV) sequences added cinematic flair to games.

## 2. Cost-Effectiveness: Economics of Production

CDs were significantly cheaper to produce than cartridges. This not only meant reduced costs for developers and publishers but also potentially lower retail prices, making games more accessible to a broader audience.

Moreover, CDs, being a standard format used across various industries, benefited from economies of scale in production.

## 3. Flexibility for Developers

The capacious nature of CDs meant that developers had more room to experiment:

- **Multiple Game Versions**: It became easier to ship games with multiple language options, catering to a global audience.

- **Patches and Updates**: Though rudimentary by today's standards, the ability to provide game patches through additional discs or PC downloads began to appear.

## 4. Multimedia Capabilities: More Than Just Games

CD-based consoles, like the PlayStation, weren't limited to just gaming. They could play music CDs, turning them into entertainment systems. This multimedia capability broadened the appeal of these consoles, making them more versatile and central in living rooms.

## 5. Load Times: The Double-Edged Sword

While CDs offered numerous benefits, they also introduced gamers to the concept of 'load times.' Unlike the almost instantaneous boot of cartridge games, CD games required some patience. However, as technology progressed, strategies to optimize and reduce these load times were developed, but they remained a notable downside of the format.

## 6. Piracy Concerns: The Unintended Consequence

CDs, for all their advantages, had a significant vulnerability: they were easier to duplicate. This led to a rise in game piracy. Many a gamer in the late 90s and early 2000s came across dubious stacks of pirated games in shady markets, leading to considerable revenue losses for developers and publishers.

The industry had to evolve, introducing various anti-piracy measures, some more effective than others.

## 7. Sealing the Fate of Cartridges

Despite their benefits, cartridges hung on for a while. Nintendo's N64, released in the heart of the CD era, persisted with cartridges, citing faster load times and reduced piracy as reasons. However, the benefits of CDs—particularly their vast storage capacity—outweighed the negatives. By the time the new millennium rolled in, most major gaming companies had transitioned to disc-based formats, marking the end of the mainstream cartridge era.

## Closing Thoughts:

The move from cartridge to CD wasn't just a technological evolution; it was a paradigm shift. It symbolized the industry's maturity, moving from bite-sized, arcade-style experiences to epic tales that rivaled movies in their scope and ambition. It was a clear message to the world: video games were no longer just child's play; they were a force to be reckoned with in the entertainment landscape.

# Benefits and Drawbacks: More Data, Longer Loading Times, and the Joy of Memory Cards

As with any seismic shift in technology, the transition from cartridges to CDs in the gaming world came with its set of advantages and drawbacks. While we basked in the glory of expansive in-game worlds and symphonic soundtracks, we also gritted our teeth during those excruciating load times. Let's dive into this mix of highs and lows.

## 1. The Upsides: All That Glitters is CD-ROM

**A. A Bigger Playground:** CDs opened the door to an entirely new level of gaming experience. The storage increase meant more substantial, more detailed, and richer worlds to explore. Gamers went from the linear levels of "Super Mario Bros." to the vast expanses of "Final Fantasy VII."

**B. Audio Excellence:** With the ability to store high-quality audio tracks, game soundtracks reached symphonic levels. This led to memorable scores, with some like "Castlevania: Symphony of the Night" achieving iconic status.

**C. Multimedia Marvel:** CD-based consoles could often play regular music CDs, allowing gamers to use their consoles as entertainment hubs, not just gaming machines.

**D. Memory Cards: Save the Day:** With games growing in complexity, the need for saving progress became paramount. Memory cards were introduced, allowing players to store game data, swap cards, and even share saved game states with friends.

## 2. The Downsides: Every Rose has its Thorn

**A. The Dreaded Load Times:** Any 90s gamer can recall the tension of waiting for a game to load, praying the screen would shift before frustration set in. This was a far cry from the almost instant playability of cartridge games.

**B. Scratches and Scuffs:** Unlike cartridges, CDs were vulnerable. A single scratch could render a game unplayable. Gone were the days when blowing into a cartridge could magically fix things.

**C. Piracy Woes:** The ease of copying CDs led to a boom in piracy. This not only hurt the industry's profits but sometimes also meant players got sub-par, glitchy versions of games.

**D. Memory Card Limitations:** As exciting as memory cards were, they had limited space. Players often had to juggle data, deciding which game saves to keep and which to overwrite. Plus, a lost memory card meant potentially hours of gameplay gone.

# 3. The Middle Ground: Mixed Blessings

**A. Game Installations:** Some games began to allow partial installations to the console's memory to reduce load times. While this made games run faster, it also consumed precious storage space.

**B. Physical vs. Digital Manuals:** CDs allowed for digital manuals to be included on-disc. While this was environmentally friendly and convenient, many gamers missed the tangible joy of flipping through a physical manual, complete with artwork and lore.

---

## Reflecting Back:

The transition from cartridge to CD was emblematic of the broader evolution of technology. It was a time of rapid innovation, where the gaming industry was finding its footing amidst its newfound possibilities and challenges. For every moment of awe at a sprawling in-game cinematic, there was a moment of annoyance at a load screen. But, in the grand tapestry of gaming history, these were the threads that wove a rich, diverse, and colorful era, setting the stage for the wonders that would follow in the 21st century.

# Remembering the First Time We Heard the PlayStation Boot-Up Sound

The year was 1995. Flannel shirts were in, "Friends" was the hottest show on television, and people were still reeling from the unexpected twists of "The Usual Suspects." But for gamers, a different kind of memory was about to be etched in their minds, one that would resonate for years, if not decades: the ethereal, almost otherworldly sound of the PlayStation booting up.

The ambiance of the room would dim, anticipation hanging thick in the air. Your fingers would lightly grace the power button, and then, as if a symphony was about to commence, it began: that iconic, synthesized crescendo, a melding of electronic tones and orchestral majesty. It wasn't just a sound—it was a portal, a gateway to uncharted digital realms.

For many, it was akin to the giddy excitement one feels just before the curtains rise at a theater. It was the promise of adventures yet to come, of battles to be fought, puzzles to be solved, and stories to unfold.

## A Personal Anecdote:

I remember visiting my cousin Jamie during the summer holidays. He was the first in our family to get a PlayStation. The living room, dappled in the golden hues of late afternoon, was filled with the scent of popcorn and the muffled sound of our parents chatting in the background.

I sat cross-legged on the carpet, controller in hand, with Jamie next to me, a mischievous grin on his face, as if he was sharing the world's greatest secret. "Ready?" he asked. I nodded, not knowing what to expect.

Then he pressed the power button.

That sound washed over us, and I swear I felt a shiver down my spine. We both looked at each other, wide-eyed, realizing we were on the cusp of something monumental. The rest of the afternoon was a blur of pixelated characters, thrilling chases, and countless retries, but that initial moment, that first ethereal note of the PlayStation's song, remained crystal clear.

---

To this day, hearing the PlayStation boot-up sound evokes a profound sense of nostalgia. It's a testament to the power of gaming, how a simple sequence of notes can transport us back to our childhood, to simpler times, to moments shared with friends and family. It wasn't just a sound. It was an anthem for an era, a rallying cry for a generation ready to embrace the future of digital entertainment.

# Chapter 3: Iconic Titles – Gaming's Hall of Fame

When we cast our minds back to the golden age of gaming, the era dominated by the PlayStation's reign, certain titles stand out not merely as games but as defining moments in our collective cultural consciousness. These were not just titles to be played; they were experiences to be lived, narratives to be unraveled, and worlds to be explored. This chapter, dear reader, is an homage to those iconic titles that shaped an era, pushing boundaries and forever cementing their places in gaming's illustrious Hall of Fame.

In the annals of video game history, every console generation brings forth a pantheon of titles that leave an indelible mark. However, the PlayStation era was distinct. It was a period of innovation, exploration, and, most crucially, storytelling. Gone were the days where gameplay was solely about jumping on platforms or shooting down space invaders. Now, gamers demanded intricate plots, multifaceted characters, and immersive worlds. The PlayStation, with its powerful hardware and CD-ROM capabilities, was poised to deliver.

Take a moment to visualize this: It's the late '90s. You're in a dimly lit room, the soft glow of a CRT television illuminating your surroundings. The PlayStation's boot-up sound—already iconic—echoes in the background. And as the game's title screen appears, you know you're about to embark on a journey. Maybe it's the dystopian streets of Midgar in "Final Fantasy VII," or perhaps it's the stealthy escapades of Solid

Snake in "Metal Gear Solid." It could even be the zany, colorful jungles with Crash Bandicoot. These were more than just digital realms; they were memories in the making.

But what truly made these titles iconic? It wasn't just their gameplay mechanics or impressive graphics, though these certainly played a part. It was the emotional resonance they carried. These games tackled themes previously untouched in this medium: love, betrayal, identity, environmental decay, and the very essence of humanity. They questioned morality, introduced us to characters with profound depth, and often left us pondering long after the credits rolled.

However, it wasn't just the narratives that were revolutionary. The PlayStation era also saw leaps in gameplay mechanics. Developers were no longer confined by the limitations of cartridges. With the expansive storage of CDs, games could be bigger, bolder, and more experimental. Levels were vast, often filled with hidden secrets and easter eggs. Gameplay mechanics diversified, offering players a range of experiences, from turn-based strategy to real-time combat, from platforming to puzzle-solving.

Couple this with the advent of the internet, and the gaming community was set ablaze. Gamers from across the globe could now connect, share experiences, trade secrets, and birth fandoms. These titles didn't just have players; they had devotees. Fans who would analyze every detail, create art, write stories, and even don costumes to bring their favorite characters to life. This was the era where games transcended their digital boundaries to influence wider pop culture.

As we delve deeper into this chapter, we'll journey through these iconic titles, revisiting their stories, their impacts, and the legacies they left behind. It's not just a trip down memory lane, but a celebration of the games that, in many ways, defined a generation. So, strap in and ready your controllers. The Hall of Fame awaits, and the legends of yesteryears beckon.

# A Nostalgic Ride Through "Final Fantasy VII"

The late '90s saw a plethora of video game releases, each vying for a spot in the limelight, but few shone as brilliantly as "Final Fantasy VII." When you utter the phrase "nostalgic ride," for many, their minds automatically wander to the expansive universe of Gaia and the adventures of Cloud Strife and his eclectic band of rebels.

## World Building and Narrative Arcs:

From the get-go, "Final Fantasy VII" set itself apart with its intricate world-building. Midgar, with its towering Mako reactors and maze-like slums, painted a vivid picture of a society divided by class and wealth. The dystopian city stood as a stark contrast to the vast and diverse landscapes players would explore later in the game, from the sun-soaked beaches of Costa Del Sol to the haunting beauty of the Forgotten City.

But the world was only a backdrop for the intricate narrative that played out. Themes of corporate greed, environmental degradation, identity crisis, love, and sacrifice were all intricately woven into the story. Each character had a purpose, a past, and a pain. There was the enigmatic Vincent, the fiercely independent Tifa, and of course, Aerith, with her tragic fate that left players reeling in shock and sorrow.

It's worth noting that while "Final Fantasy VII" was adored for its innovative gameplay and storyline, it also paved the way for its successor, "Final Fantasy VIII." This follow-up explored themes of love, war, and memory, with its own captivating characters and moments. Though it stood distinct, "VIII" surely owed part of its DNA to the brilliance that "VII" had introduced.

## Breaking Barriers in Game Mechanics and Design:

The Materia system was another defining feature. It provided layers of strategy, allowing players to customize their characters in unique ways. This flexibility ensured that no two playthroughs were the same. Battles were a delicate dance of strategy, with players often having to rethink their approach depending on the opponent.

Graphically, "Final Fantasy VII" was a revelation. Full-motion videos blended seamlessly with gameplay, creating cinematic experiences that, at the time, were unparalleled. Summons, like the awe-inducing Knights of the Round, were visual masterpieces that players would often cast just to marvel at the spectacle.

## Cultural Impact and Legacy:

"Final Fantasy VII" wasn't just a game; it was a cultural phenomenon. It introduced a generation to the potential of gaming as a storytelling medium. Conversations around schoolyards, water coolers, and forums were abuzz with theories, strategies, and shared experiences. And who could forget the countless debates on THAT Aerith scene? The game's impact resonated far beyond the confines of the PlayStation console.

## A Personal Anecdote:

I recall one cold winter's evening, the room lit only by the flickering screen of my old CRT television. I was navigating Cloud and his party through the snowfields, trying to find my way to the next town. My younger sister sat beside me, wrapped in a blanket, her eyes wide with wonder at the pixelated landscapes and the creatures that roamed them. She wasn't there to play but to experience the story.

As the hours waned and the night deepened, we reached the City of the Ancients. The haunting melodies, the ethereal glow of the crystalline structures—it was all mesmerizing. But nothing prepared us for what was to come. As the events with Aerith unfolded, my sister and I sat in stunned silence. The room was cold, but the tears that streamed down our faces were hot.

In that moment, it wasn't just a game. It was a shared experience, a story that evoked profound emotion. It was a testament to the game's power, its ability to bridge the gap between digital polygons and raw human emotion. We talked about it for days, finding solace in shared forums with strangers who felt that same piercing pain, that shared sense of loss.

To this day, when the opening notes of Aerith's theme play, it evokes memories of that night. It serves as a poignant reminder of the power of storytelling, of shared experiences, and of the bond forged between two siblings over a shared tragedy in a digital realm.

---

In retrospect, "Final Fantasy VII" was more than just a game. It was a narrative masterpiece that redefined what video games could achieve. It blurred the lines between player and character, reality and fiction, evoking emotions and leaving an indelible mark on all who journeyed through its vast world.

# Crash Bandicoot: From Wumpa Islands to Sequel Delights

There's a saying that goes: "You can't teach an old Bandicoot new tricks." But what if that Bandicoot is spinning, jumping, and navigating treacherous terrains while dodging TNT crates? Enter Crash Bandicoot, the zany, denim shorts-wearing marsupial that captured hearts and became the unofficial mascot for a generation of PlayStation enthusiasts.

## Wumpa Fruit and Whacky Antics: The Innovation of the First Chapter

Back in a world pre-Crash, platform games had a certain predictability. Most had a side-scrolling perspective, allowing players to move their character left or right. Then, in a move as radical as Crash's dance moves, Naughty Dog decided, "Hey, what if we spun this whole idea around? Literally." And just like that, the '3D' platformer as we knew it was born.

Crash Bandicoot was innovative in its approach, shifting from the typical side-scrolling view to a behind-the-character perspective, a kind of 'forward-scrolling' if you will. Gamers weren't just moving left and right anymore; they were moving into the screen, away from the screen, and occasionally side-to-side for good measure. It was a wild, roller-coaster of a ride, filled with lush jungles, dangerous mines, and high-stake chases. The objective? Well, rescue the damsel in distress (Tawna Bandicoot), take down the evil Dr. Neo Cortex, and consume as many Wumpa fruits as possible along the way.

It was clear that the game didn't take itself too seriously. The enemies weren't just generic baddies; they were skunks with attitude problems, turtles that defied gravity, and venus fly traps with indigestion issues. And the bosses? Let's just say battling a mutated kangaroo with a penchant for boxing gloves isn't something you see every day. Or ever.

## Sequels, Sequins, and Spin-offs: Crash's Extended Family

With the undeniable success of the first game, it was only a matter of time before the world demanded more of our orange, furry friend. And oh, did Naughty Dog deliver!

**"Crash Bandicoot 2: Cortex Strikes Back"** was the equivalent of a movie sequel that's better than the original. Sorry, "Godfather Part II." While Crash's signature moves remained intact (because why fix what ain't broken?), the sequel introduced new mechanics. Slide attacks, high jumps, body slams—the Bandicoot was clearly taking his gym membership seriously. The narrative also delved deeper. Sure, Cortex was back with a so-called 'plan to save the world,' but we all knew his PhD in deception wasn't just for show.

Next came **"Crash Bandicoot: Warped"** which, by the way, wasn't just a comment on Crash's mental state, but a nod to the time-traveling antics our hero would get up to. Ever seen a Bandicoot ride a baby T-Rex or joust in medieval times? No? Well, Warped made sure you did. This game was the zaniest of the trilogy, stretching the bounds of both time and sanity. And let's not forget the iconic motorcycle levels, because nothing says '90s cool' quite like a Bandicoot on a bike, racing against time (literally).

But it wasn't just mainline games that Crash graced us with. Spin-offs like **"Crash Team Racing"** proved that Mario wasn't the only one who could throw a karting party. Combining tight controls, memorable tracks, and that signature Crash craziness, CTR became a multiplayer favorite, proving once and for all that Bandicoots drive better than Italian plumbers.

## A Nod to the Nuttiness:

It's easy to dismiss the Crash Bandicoot series as 'just another platformer,' but to do so would be to overlook its genius. Naughty Dog took a genre that was becoming predictable and turned it on its head. Through innovative game design, hilarious characters, and a level of challenge that had many of us chucking our controllers in frustration (High Road, anyone?), Crash Bandicoot cemented its place in the gaming Hall of Fame.

And let's be honest: In a world filled with grim, gritty, and hyper-realistic titles, isn't it refreshing to have a game where a Bandicoot can thwart the plans of an evil scientist, all while wearing a pair of sneakers and jorts? Crash taught us that it's okay to be different, to be a little zany, and to spin through life with unbridled enthusiasm. So, here's to the orange marsupial who leaped into our lives, spinning, dancing, and laughing all the way. After all, in the wise words of Crash himself: "Whoa!"

# Metal Gear Solid: Espionage, Intrigue, and the Magic of Hideo Kojima

In the realm of gaming, few titles have left an indelible mark quite like "Metal Gear Solid" (MGS). It's a name that doesn't just represent a game but an entire movement in storytelling, gameplay, and sheer artistic ambition. Stealth, espionage, political drama, and cardboard boxes — it's a cocktail only Hideo Kojima could've mixed.

## Narrative Depth and Mind-Bending Plots

Diving into the world of MGS was never just about playing a game. It was an experience — a dive into a narrative so rich, so convoluted, and so engrossing that you'd find yourself scribbling notes, piecing together the lore, and diving into forums deep into the night. Set against a backdrop of nuclear disarmament and shadow organizations, players took on the role of Solid Snake, an elite operative tasked with averting global catastrophe.

Yet, the magic of MGS wasn't just in its overarching plot, but in the details. Codec conversations, Easter eggs, and nuanced character development made the world feel alive. Every character, from the stoic Revolver Ocelot to the tragic Sniper Wolf, had depth, motivation, and complexity.

## Gameplay Innovation: Tactical Espionage Action

While the narrative was a powerful driving force, gameplay was where MGS truly broke the mold. Stealth wasn't just an option; it was a necessity. Instead of charging in guns blazing, players had to think, strategize, and often retreat into that iconic cardboard box. This approach to gameplay was revolutionary at the time, turning traditional action game mechanics on their head.

Kojima and his team played with the medium in ways previously unthinkable. Remember the Psycho Mantis encounter? Players had to physically switch their controller ports to beat this psychic foe, a meta-gameplay trick that left jaws on the floor.

## The Genius of Hideo Kojima

Behind every twist, every heart-wrenching moment, and every innovative gameplay mechanic was the mastermind Hideo Kojima. Kojima's approach to game design wasn't just about mechanics or graphics; it was holistic. He viewed games as a medium for storytelling on par with cinema, and MGS was his magnum opus.

Kojima's storytelling wasn't just about forwarding a plot but about conveying emotions, exploring philosophical themes, and making players question their own role within the game. It's no wonder he's often referred to as the 'auteur' of the gaming world, drawing parallels with iconic filmmakers like Kubrick or Tarantino.

## A Personal Anecdote:

It was a cold winter afternoon when I first booted up "Metal Gear Solid." I'd heard the rumors, the hushed conversations about its brilliance, but nothing could prepare me for what lay ahead. I remember the tension of sneaking past guards, the adrenaline rush of close calls, and the sheer awe of the unfolding narrative.

One moment, in particular, stands out. It was the scene where Sniper Wolf and Snake face off in a snowy field. The weight of the moment, the haunting background score, and the melancholic dialogue made it more than just a boss fight. I remember my hands shaking, not just from the challenge but from the emotional weight of the encounter. Once it was over, I had to pause the game, step outside, and take a few deep breaths. No game had ever evoked such a visceral reaction from me.

That night, I dreamt of Shadow Moses Island, of its dark hallways and snow-covered plains. I was Solid Snake, not just playing him. That's the magic of "Metal Gear Solid" — it transcends the screen, immersing players in a world so real that the line between game and reality blurs.

## Legacy and Impact

"Metal Gear Solid" isn't just a game; it's a legacy. It challenged the conventions of gaming, proving that video games could be as emotionally resonant and thought-provoking as any film or novel. MGS spawned sequels, prequels, spin-offs, and even a dedicated fan base that dissects every detail, every theory, every nuance of Kojima's creation.

In the annals of gaming history, "Metal Gear Solid" will always stand as a testament to what's possible when a visionary creator, a dedicated team, and an immersive medium come together. It's not just tactical espionage action; it's a masterclass in game design, storytelling, and artistic expression.

In the words of Solid Snake himself, "I'm no hero... Never was. I'm just an old killer, hired to do some wet work." But for millions around the world, Snake, and the world Kojima crafted, will forever remain iconic heroes in the pantheon of gaming.

# Gran Turismo: Revving Up the Racing Game Genre

The world of video game racing before "Gran Turismo" (GT) was certainly entertaining. We had arcade racers and rally games, pixelated cars and simple tracks, but what we didn't have was realism. Enter "Gran Turismo," the game that didn't just want you to race cars but to **feel** them, to understand them, to truly immerse yourself in the world of automotive engineering and racing finesse. It was a paradigm shift, not just a game.

## An Ode to Realism: Steering Away from Arcade

Before GT graced our screens, many racing games leaned heavily into the arcade style. The focus was primarily on speed, flashy visuals, and less about the authenticity of the racing experience. "Gran Turismo" turned this model on its head. Instead of offering merely a game, it presented a simulation.

The game's tagline, "The Real Driving Simulator," wasn't just marketing speak. It encapsulated everything the game set out to be. From the roar of the engines to the grip of the tires on different tarmac surfaces, the game pursued an almost obsessive level of detail. Each car behaved as its real-world counterpart would, with unique handling, acceleration, and braking characteristics. For the first time, gamers were required to think about brake timing, tire wear, weight distribution, and a myriad of other factors that real drivers contend with.

## A Car Lover's Dream: The Sheer Volume of Choices

"Gran Turismo" was ambitious, not just in its gameplay mechanics but in its content. The game boasted an impressive roster of cars, with hundreds of models from various manufacturers. And it wasn't just about flashy supercars; everything from everyday sedans to iconic racing models found its place in the game.

This comprehensive car list turned many gamers into car enthusiasts and vice versa. It wasn't unusual to find players spending hours in the game's garage, tweaking their vehicles, testing different parts, and hunting for that elusive perfect tuning setup.

## From Motor Toon to Gran Turismo: An Evolution

Before delving deeper into the intricacies of GT, it's worth taking a detour to Polyphony Digital's earlier title, "Motor Toon Grand Prix 2." A world away from the realism of GT, "Motor Toon Grand Prix 2" was a quirky, cartoonish racer, reminiscent more of "Mario Kart" than anything else. Characters with oversized heads raced in vibrant, imaginative tracks, using power-ups to outwit their competitors.

So, how does a developer go from cartoon racing to the pinnacle of racing realism? It all comes down to vision and ambition. While "Motor Toon Grand Prix 2" showcased Polyphony Digital's ability to create a fun, engaging racer, "Gran Turismo" demonstrated their depth, their commitment to craft, and their passion for automobiles.

## Kazunori Yamauchi: The Man Behind the Wheel

No discussion about "Gran Turismo" would be complete without mentioning its creator, Kazunori Yamauchi. A car enthusiast himself, Yamauchi's passion for automobiles and racing was the driving force behind GT's creation. He envisioned a game where players didn't just race cars but lived and breathed them.

Yamauchi's leadership and passion were evident in every aspect of the game. From the meticulous modeling of each car to the accurate representation of various world tracks, his fingerprints were everywhere. His dedication to detail even led him to personally test drive some of the cars featured in the game, ensuring the in-game experience was as close to real life as possible.

Under Yamauchi's guidance, "Gran Turismo" didn't just become a game but a brand, a legacy, and a touchstone for racing enthusiasts worldwide. Subsequent iterations of the game pushed the boundaries further, but the core ethos remained unchanged: an unwavering commitment to realism, authenticity, and the love of cars.

## In Conclusion: The Legacy of Gran Turismo

Looking back, "Gran Turismo" was more than just a game. It was a movement. It transformed the way we looked at racing games, shifting the focus from arcade fun to immersive simulation. It introduced an entire generation to the nuances of automotive engineering, the thrill of tuning, and the sheer joy of racing.

"Gran Turismo" wasn't just about winning races; it was about understanding cars, respecting them, and truly experiencing the world of racing. In doing so, it set the gold standard for racing simulations, a standard that remains unmatched to this day.

# Tomb Raider: More Than Just Pixels and Pyramids

Ah, "Tomb Raider"! Who could forget the iconic, dual-pistol-wielding, acrobatic archaeologist with a penchant for spelunking in dangerous ancient ruins and a wardrobe that, let's admit it, wasn't entirely practical for said activities? But beyond her pixelated physique and gravity-defying stunts, Lara Croft became an emblem of the gaming industry and shaped pop culture in ways that few other game characters have managed.

## From Tombs to TV Screens: A Gaming Revolution

When "Tomb Raider" debuted in 1996, it wasn't just introducing a new game; it was pioneering an entire genre. The blend of action, adventure, puzzle-solving, and exploration set against a captivating backstory set the game apart. Players weren't just controlling Lara; they were embarking on globe-trotting adventures, deciphering ancient mysteries, and battling foes ranging from dangerous wildlife to supernatural entities.

And let's not forget the awe-inspiring environments. While today's gamers might chuckle at the blocky graphics of the original game, back then, those 3D levels—from the dark caves of Peru to the majestic Great Pyramid—were groundbreaking.

## Lara Croft: The Unlikely Pop Icon

It's one thing for a video game character to be popular within the gaming community. It's an entirely different ballgame to transcend that sphere and become a mainstream icon. Yet, that's precisely what Lara Croft did. With her confident stride, signature braid, and, of course, those unforgettable... ahem, dual pistols, she became more than just a digital character; she became a symbol of female empowerment in a predominantly male gaming world.

Yes, there were debates about her design and whether she was a figure of empowerment or objectification. But as the series evolved, so did Lara. She became more fleshed out (no pun intended), her character given depth, backstory, and vulnerabilities. By the time we got to the reboots, she was a multi-dimensional character, showcasing both strength and emotional depth, making her relatable and genuine.

## The Wider Impact: Films, Merchandise, and a Place in The Louvre

Let's face it; when your video game character gets portrayed by Angelina Jolie on the big screen, you know you've made it. "Tomb Raider" was no longer confined to the realm of consoles and PCs. Lara was everywhere - action figures, comic books, theme park rides, and even stamps. Yep, she's that big of a deal.

Perhaps the most ironic (and impressive) feat was when a character who spent her life raiding tombs and pilfering artifacts was commemorated in an exhibition at The Louvre. That's right—the museum that houses the Mona Lisa once celebrated the digital raider of ancient artifacts. Talk about life coming full circle!

## Jokes and Jibes: We've All Had Our Lara Moments

Remember that time you tried to emulate Lara's swan dive in the pool and ended up belly-flopping instead? Or when you thought wearing a backpack and sunglasses indoors would make you look adventurous, but you just resembled a lost tourist? We've all been there.

And let's not forget those hours spent trying to maneuver Lara into the right position just to jump across a simple ledge. You'd think an archaeologist with her skill set would've mastered basic jumping, right? Well, if she had, half of us would've finished the game in a few hours instead of a few weeks. So, thanks, Lara, for keeping us entertained (and frustrated)!

## A Legacy Set in Stone (and Pixels)

In the vast world of gaming, few characters have achieved the kind of widespread recognition and influence as Lara Croft.

From her digital origins to her impact on movies, merchandise, and even high culture, she's been a force to be reckoned with.

But beyond the fame, the merchandise, and the debates, "Tomb Raider" gave us something invaluable: adventures. Adventures that transported us to lost civilizations, taught us the value of perseverance (especially during those tricky jumps), and introduced us to a heroine who, despite her flaws and pixelated origins, became an icon for the ages.

So, here's to Lara Croft—the archaeologist who made us all dream of adventure, even if the closest we ever got to a tomb was our basement! Cheers!

# Tekken: A Fistful of Fights, Family Feuds, and Fanciful Characters

When it comes to 3D fighting games, few franchises boast the longevity, intricacy, and compelling narrative of the "Tekken" series. Emerging from the arcades of the 1990s to the living rooms across the globe, the game has seen many iterations and has built a loyal fan base over the decades. Let's take a trip down memory lane and revisit the highs and lows (and uppercuts and sidesteps) of this iconic fighting game.

## Tekken's Humble Beginnings: Insert Coin to Fight

"Tekken" arrived at a time when fighting games were thriving, with the likes of "Street Fighter" and "Mortal Kombat" already commanding the arcades. Yet, Namco's "Tekken" stood out. Why? It was one of the first games to fully embrace the third dimension, allowing sidesteps, and more strategic gameplay. No longer were players restricted to a two-dimensional plane; the fight had depth, both literally and figuratively.

## The Mishima Saga: It's All in the Family

At its core, "Tekken" revolves around the turbulent and often violent Mishima family saga. A tale of power struggles, betrayals, and quite frankly, questionable parenting choices, the series' narrative is as compelling as its gameplay. Each installment delves deeper into the twisted relationships between Heihachi, his son Kazuya, grandson Jin, and other family members, often culminating in a throwdown of epic proportions atop a cliff or a volcano. You know, typical family reunion spots.

## A Diverse Roster: From Boxing Kangaroos to Luchadores

What truly makes "Tekken" shine is its wildly diverse roster of fighters. And we do mean **wild**. Sure, there are traditional martial artists, but then there's also a boxing kangaroo (Roger), a fighting bear (Kuma), and let's not forget the wood-made combatant Mokujin. Yoshimitsu, a sort of cyber samurai with a flair for the dramatic, stands out as one of the most uniquely designed characters in fighting game history. Each character, bizarre or not, has its own distinctive fighting style, backstory, and reason to enter the King of Iron Fist Tournament.

## Mechanics and Mastery: Deep Gameplay for the Dedicated

"Tekken" is both accessible for newcomers and deep for veterans. While beginners can mash buttons and pull off impressive-looking moves, mastery of the game is an art. It demands understanding of frame data, precise timing, juggles, and character-specific combos. This depth has led to "Tekken" becoming a mainstay in competitive esports scenes, with tournaments held worldwide.

## The Journey of the Series: From Pixel Punches to Detailed Duels

While the core mechanics of "Tekken" remained consistent, the series has evolved dramatically in terms of graphics and presentation. "Tekken 7," for instance, introduced the Rage Art system, allowing players to make comebacks when their health is low. Graphically, from the blocky characters of the first installment to the detailed, almost lifelike fighters of the latest games, the evolution is nothing short of breathtaking.

## A Legacy of Fights and More Fights

Across its many iterations—including main series titles and spin-offs like "Tekken Tag Tournament"—"Tekken" has always managed to stay fresh and relevant. Whether it's the introduction of new mechanics, the ongoing saga of the Mishima family, or the thrill of learning a new character, there's always a reason for players to return to the arena.

In conclusion, "Tekken" isn't just another fighting game; it's a testament to how a combination of compelling storytelling, deep gameplay mechanics, and a dash of the bizarre can create a franchise that stands the test of time. Whether you're team Heihachi or team Jin, or even if you're just there for the pandas and kangaroos, there's no denying that "Tekken" has left an indelible mark on the world of gaming. Now, get ready for the next battle!

# How These Games Transformed Gaming Narratives and Mechanics

In the golden era of gaming marked by the PlayStation's reign, titles like "Final Fantasy VII," "Crash Bandicoot," "Metal Gear Solid," "Gran Turismo," "Tomb Raider," and "Tekken" were not merely pastimes. They were revolutions in digital storytelling and gameplay mechanics, setting benchmarks for future games. Let's dive into how these icons reshaped the gaming landscape.

## Narrative Depth and World-building

Prior to the PlayStation era, games often had straightforward stories or sometimes none at all. However, titles like "Final Fantasy VII" raised the narrative bar. No longer were games just about reaching the end; they were about experiencing heart-wrenching stories, developing connections with characters, and exploring richly detailed worlds. Cloud Strife's journey wasn't just a mission; it was an emotional roller-coaster filled with love, loss, and revelations.

Similarly, "Metal Gear Solid" brought cinematic storytelling to gaming, complete with intricate plots, deep philosophical musings, and memorable characters. Snake's stealthy escapades weren't just missions—they were politically charged narratives exploring the ethics of warfare and human nature.

## Breaking the Mould with Mechanics

Mechanically, each game brought something new to the table. "Crash Bandicoot" transformed the traditional platformer with its dynamic camera angles and challenging level designs. "Gran Turismo" wasn't just about speed; it was about the love for cars, the thrill of the drive, and the precision required to master each turn.

"Tekken" introduced a 3D fighting plane, allowing for a more strategic combat approach, while "Tomb Raider" merged action, puzzle-solving, and exploration, offering players a multi-faceted gaming experience.

## Character Depth and Development

Gone were the days of one-dimensional characters. Lara Croft became a symbol of empowerment, enduring various challenges, not just as a game character but as an icon in the broader media landscape. The members of the Mishima family in "Tekken" showcased deep-rooted familial issues, making players invest emotionally in their fates.

## Gameplay Evolution and User Experience

The move from cartridges to CDs allowed for expansive games filled with content. It also meant more elaborate soundtracks, voice acting, and cinematic cutscenes, making games feel more like interactive movies.

Additionally, games began to implement mechanics that responded to player choices. "Metal Gear Solid" rewarded stealth over aggression, and games like "Final Fantasy VII" offered branching narratives and multiple endings based on player decisions.

## Influencing Future Generations

The ripple effects of these iconic games can still be felt today. Open-world exploration, intricate narratives, moral choice systems, and realistic gameplay mechanics—all can trace their lineage back to these PlayStation classics.

In essence, these games did more than just entertain; they transformed expectations. They proved that games could be art, that digital worlds could evoke genuine emotion, and that players could be more than just passive participants—they could be co-authors of unforgettable stories. The PlayStation era didn't just redefine gaming; it elevated it, ushering in a new age where games became narratives that resonated, evolved, and inspired.

# The Birth of Fan Communities and the Early Internet Days

Ah, the early days of the internet! A time when you had to ensure no one was on the phone before you could connect, and the familiar screech of a dial-up modem was the gateway to a new digital frontier. As the World Wide Web began to weave its intricate tapestry, video games, especially the iconic titles of the PlayStation era, found a new avenue to build and sustain communities. Let's take a pixelated trip back to the birth of fan communities in these embryonic internet days.

## Forums, Chat Rooms, and GeoCities

Before the sleek, responsive websites of today, we had GeoCities. Fans, armed with a passion for their favorite games and a basic understanding of HTML, built dedicated fan sites. These sites, adorned with animated GIFs and MIDI versions of game soundtracks, became sanctuaries for fellow enthusiasts.

Forums and chat rooms were the social media platforms of yesteryears. Places like GameFAQs became essential for gamers, not just for the cheats or walkthroughs, but for the message boards where fans debated, theorized, and gushed about their favorite games.

## Fan Theories and Fanfictions

The narratives of games like "Final Fantasy VII" or "Metal Gear Solid" were intricate, leaving plenty of room for interpretation. Fans took to the internet to share their theories, some wild, some plausible, and some that were so well thought out that they seemed almost canon.

Alongside theories, the internet saw the birth of fanfiction. Fans crafted their own stories, giving side characters more screen time or exploring "what if" scenarios. These fan-made narratives not only showcased the fans' creativity but deepened the lore and enriched the community's bond.

## Early Days of Cosplay and Fan Art

While fan art and cosplay might seem commonplace now, the early internet days were crucial in their proliferation. Websites dedicated to showcasing fan-made art became increasingly popular. Players took their admiration for characters like Lara Croft and Jin Kazama off-screen, recreating their iconic looks in painstaking detail.

## Game Mods and the Dawn of User-Generated Content

The PlayStation era coincided with the early days of game modding. Fans, not content with just playing, started tweaking games, adding new skins, levels, or even entirely new gameplay mechanics. These mods, shared over the internet, laid the groundwork for today's user-generated content.

## The Rise of Online Multiplayer and Clans

Although the PlayStation wasn't primarily known for online gaming, the seeds of online multiplayer communities were sown during this period. Early PC games started experimenting with online modes, setting the stage for the PlayStation's successors and the rise of online gaming communities.

## Conclusion: The Interconnected Gaming World

The combination of the PlayStation's groundbreaking titles and the early days of the internet created a perfect storm for fan communities' birth. These communities, which started as small pockets of dedicated fans on rudimentary websites, have now blossomed into massive, interconnected networks spanning the globe. They're a testament to the lasting impact of the games of this era and the unifying power of the internet. In these pixelated corridors of the web, lifelong friendships were formed, epic tales were shared, and the foundation for today's gaming culture was solidly laid.

# Chapter 4: The Rivals Respond

Ah, the 90s! A time of baggy jeans, questionable hair choices, and in the world of gaming, an all-out console war. As Sony nonchalantly waltzed into the video gaming arena, flaunting its swanky PlayStation and wooing gamers left and right, the established bigwigs of the industry sat up and took notice. Imagine being Nintendo and Sega—companies that had been playing tug-of-war for video game dominance—and suddenly, out of the blue, here comes Sony with its shiny new CD-based console, acting like they own the place. The audacity!

Sony's PlayStation was the new kid on the block, but it was no pushover. Its rapid success was like that of a new pop star skyrocketing to the top of the charts, leaving the old guard—those long-established rock bands—to rethink their strategies. Nintendo and Sega, while once fierce rivals, now found themselves facing a common threat. But as they say, competition breeds innovation, and boy, did it deliver.

Now, if we peek behind the corporate curtains, the 90s were rife with boardroom dramas worthy of a soap opera. Did you know that the PlayStation's origin story is rooted in a failed collaboration between Sony and Nintendo? Oh yes, dear reader! The PlayStation could have been a Nintendo console. In the early 90s, Sony and Nintendo briefly held hands, dreaming of a CD-ROM add-on for the Super Nintendo. But, like a twist in a Shakespearean tragedy, the partnership soured, and Sony, perhaps with a hint of vengeance in its eyes, decided to go solo. The rest, as they say, is history.

Sega, on the other hand, had its own pot of corporate shenanigans brewing. Amidst internal disagreements and a slew of different hardware releases, the company was juggling the Saturn, the 32X, and the Sega CD—often to the confusion of their own fanbase. With PlayStation's entry, the stakes were higher than ever. Sega had to pull a rabbit out of its hat, or maybe a blue hedgehog?

But it wasn't just about hardware. The software—the games—had to shine. As PlayStation birthed iconic titles, the competition scrambled, leading to an explosion of creativity and some of the best games the industry has ever seen.

So, buckle up as we embark on this corporate roller-coaster, diving deep into how Sony's rivals responded to the PlayStation's disruptive entrance. Through a maze of strategic moves, blunders, alliances, and betrayals, we'll explore how the titans of gaming tackled the PlayStation challenge. Expect drama, expect innovation, and maybe, just maybe, expect a bit of irony because, in the world of corporate video gaming, the game never truly ends—it just gets a sequel.

# Sega's Saturn and Dreamcast: Innovative but Unfortunate

The 1990s was a transformative decade in the world of gaming, a veritable Wild West of consoles vying for the top spot. And in this battle of silicon and pixels, Sega stood as a formidable contender, driven by innovation and, at times, sheer audacity. Yet, in the intricate dance of corporate strategy, market readiness, and a sprinkle of sheer luck, even the mightiest can falter.

## A Bit of SEGA History

To understand the trajectory of the Saturn and Dreamcast, it's essential to first dive into the storied past of Sega itself. Founded in the 1940s as Service Games, SEGA (an acronym of the name) began its journey in Hawaii, providing coin-operated amusement machines for military bases. From these modest beginnings, the company expanded and eventually moved to Tokyo, Japan, transitioning into the video game industry in the 1970s.

By the 1980s, SEGA had become a household name, chiefly due to the phenomenal success of its arcade games. However, it was the 16-bit era, particularly with the Sega Genesis (or Mega Drive outside of North America), that truly set the stage for SEGA's console aspirations. Under the leadership of Tom Kalinske, Sega of America's President and CEO from 1990 to 1996, the company adopted a fearless and sometimes brash marketing strategy, positioning the Genesis as the edgier alternative to Nintendo's family-friendly image. With the iconic "Genesis does what Nintendon't" campaign and the birth of Sonic the Hedgehog, SEGA's star was on the rise.

## The Saturn Odyssey

With the success of the Genesis behind them, the Saturn was SEGA's answer to the burgeoning 32-bit era. Released in 1994 in Japan and a year later in the West, it boasted dual CPUs and an architecture built for both 2D and 3D graphics. Yet, despite games like "Virtua Fighter" and "Panzer Dragoon" showcasing its potential, the Saturn's journey was fraught with challenges.

The console's unexpected early launch in North America surprised not just consumers but developers and retailers. This decision, while intended to give SEGA a head start over its competition, backfired spectacularly. With developers caught off-guard, game releases were sparse. Retailers, feeling snubbed, were reluctant to give the Saturn prime shelf space.

## Dreamcast's Dreamy Debut and Sudden Descent

The Dreamcast, launching in 1998 (Japan) and 1999 (Western markets), was SEGA's answer to its previous missteps and a leap into the future. This console, with its in-built modem, hinted at the dawn of online gaming. It saw titles like "Shenmue" push the boundaries of what games could be.

However, just as the Dreamcast was picking up steam, the looming shadow of Sony's PlayStation 2—with its promise of advanced graphics and DVD playback capabilities—cast a dark cloud over SEGA's dreams. For many gamers, the allure of the PS2 was just too strong.

## Tom Kalinske and the SEGA Spirit

A significant figure during SEGA's rise was Tom Kalinske, whose bold strategies with the Genesis had once given Nintendo a run for its money. Kalinske, with his outside-the-box thinking, championed aggressive marketing campaigns and cultivated key partnerships, like the one with Electronic Arts. However, with the Saturn, even his expertise couldn't navigate the challenges presented by the surprise launch and internal disagreements with SEGA's Japanese division.

## A Personal Anecdote

I remember the first time I laid my hands on a Dreamcast. A friend, whose dad always seemed to have the latest gadgets, invited me over. As the console booted up and I heard that iconic swirl sound, a sense of excitement filled the room. We spent hours playing "Sonic Adventure," completely engrossed in the vibrant world of the blue hedgehog. Later, as the sun set, we took on the streets of "Crazy Taxi," laughing at our abysmal driving skills.

It wasn't just about the graphics or the gameplay; it was the experience. That day, the Dreamcast felt like a window into the future. It's heartbreaking, in retrospect, to know that such a promising console would see an early exit.

## The End of an Era

The Saturn and Dreamcast, for all their innovation, faced the unforgiving realities of the market. By 2001, SEGA, making a difficult decision, pivoted from hardware to software, marking the end of its console era. Yet, while these consoles are often remembered for their misfortunes, they embody the spirit of SEGA—a company that, time and time again, dared to dream big.

# Nintendo's 64-bit Answer: GoldenEye, Mario, and Cartridges

During the 1990s, when Sony and SEGA played their disc-based symphony, there was another orchestra tuning its instruments in a corner. A well-known maestro, Nintendo, was prepping to give its answer to the CD-driven clamor. And the name of their response? The Nintendo 64.

## The Birth of a New Era

After dominating with the Super Nintendo, there was palpable excitement about Nintendo's next move. Unlike Sony and SEGA, Nintendo zigged when others zagged. They chose cartridges over CDs. Why? Speed. Cartridges had minimal load times, a luxury CDs didn't offer. However, this decision was a double-edged sword, as we'll soon discover.

## The Legend Returns: Super Mario 64

When the Nintendo 64 was unveiled in 1996, it had a secret weapon: a plump, mustached plumber named Mario. But this wasn't the Mario we knew. He was no longer confined to two dimensions. "Super Mario 64" was a watershed moment. Gamers could freely run around in lush 3D environments, from the serene "Bob-omb Battlefield" to the haunting halls of "Big Boo's Haunt."

Every jump, every punch, every star collected was an epiphany. Mario's agility, coupled with the analog stick on the N64's controller, meant players had an unparalleled level of precision. Nintendo had not just released a game; they had redefined platformers.

## FPS Brilliance: GoldenEye 007

On a console studded with gems, Rare's "GoldenEye 007" shone brightly. The world of first-person shooters, hitherto a PC stronghold, was now accessible to console gamers. The narrative? Engaging. The gameplay? Stellar. The multiplayer? Addictive. Many a friendship was tested over split-screen deathmatches, proximity mines in Facility being a particular favorite (or bane).

GoldenEye proved that the FPS genre had a home on consoles. Its legacy, both in its gameplay mechanics and multiplayer approach, can still be felt in today's titles.

## Cartridges: A Blessing and a Curse

While cartridges ensured that games loaded at the speed of light, they came with baggage. First, they were more expensive to produce than CDs. This cost, inevitably, was passed on to consumers. Then there was the capacity issue. Cartridges held less data compared to CDs. Developers had to compress audio and visual assets, sometimes at the cost of quality.

Several game developers, finding these limitations restricting, chose to jump ship. One notable example is Square, which took its "Final Fantasy" series to the PlayStation, citing CDs' capacity as a primary reason.

## Conclusion

The Nintendo 64, with its unique controller, powerful graphics, and memorable games, is fondly remembered. It was a testament to Nintendo's philosophy: gameplay over graphics, fun over form. In an era where CD was king, the N64 rode in on its cartridge-steed, proving that in the world of gaming, innovation and quality always have a fighting chance.

# The Console Wars Heat Up: Marketing, Fan Battles, and "My Console's Better Than Yours"

The 90s, folks! An era of frosted tips, dial-up modems, and... console wars? That's right, beneath the calm exterior of boy bands and slap bracelets, a storm was brewing in the world of gaming. Two titans (and a few daring challengers) were duking it out, not just in hardware specs, but in sassy ads, playground debates, and more than a few passive-aggressive jabs.

## A War of Words (and Ads)

Anyone remember SEGA's "Genesis does what Nintendon't"? Oh, SEGA went there. It was less of a sales pitch and more of a challenge thrown in the face of their rivals. Not to be outdone, Sony entered the arena with their famous "U R Not E" campaign for the PlayStation, a clever nod to how 'e'dgy they were. Remember, this was the 90s. Edge was everything.

Nintendo, traditionally the more "family-friendly" company, usually stayed above the fray... publicly. Behind the scenes, however, they were known to be fiercely competitive. Ever wonder why "Rare," the makers of 'GoldenEye' and 'Donkey Kong 64', shifted allegiance to Microsoft? Rumor has it that internal disputes with Nintendo might've been a driving factor.

## Playground Politics

Before the age of social media flame wars, the real battlegrounds were schoolyards. Conversations ran hot with statements like, "Mario could totally beat Sonic in a race!" or "Cloud Strife's Buster Sword could cut Mega Drive in half!" Factual accuracy wasn't the main concern; it was about defending your console's honor, even if it meant questioning the integrity of another's Pokémon card collection.

## The Sneaky Side of the War

Did you know Sony and Nintendo were almost allies? That's right, they initially collaborated on a CD-ROM add-on for the Super Nintendo. But corporate disagreements led to a spectacular breakup, and the rest is history. Now, imagine a world where Mario and Crash Bandicoot could've been roommates. Mind-bending, right?

SEGA, in their drive to be the "cool kid", sometimes went too far. They secretly funded focus groups not just to improve their products, but to pinpoint and amplify the weaknesses of competitors. Sneaky? Absolutely. Effective? Jury's still out on that one.

## A Blessing in Disguise

The fiercest competition often leads to the most innovation. The console wars propelled technology forward at an unprecedented rate. From SEGA's audacious move to release the Saturn early (a strategy that backfired, but hey, points for boldness) to Sony's introduction of the DualShock controller, shaking up the way we literally felt games, this era was rife with daring moves.

## In Conclusion: The Warriors Rest

While the 90s console war was filled with drama, irony, and more than a little pettiness, it's essential to remember the good that came out of it. Gamers got a front-row seat to technological evolution, and the industry matured. And, for a generation, it offered an invaluable life lesson: it's okay for someone to be wrong about which console is best, as long as you remember that your chosen one is superior. Always. ●

# Chapter 5: Gaming Gets Social

In the sprawling landscape of today, socializing doesn't just mean catching up over coffee or attending a Sunday brunch. It's sending your friend a digital heart after they've run 5 miles, sharing memes that cater to the niche-est of your interests, or discussing the strategy behind the latest raid in an MMORPG. It's a world where being "online" is almost synonymous with being alive, and where our social interactions are frequently punctuated with pings, tweets, and notifications.

But before this always-connected, tweet-driven era, there was another kind of revolution taking place, a seismic shift that would pave the way for the hyper-connected reality we're part of today. It was a time when gaming began its journey from solitary pastime to social phenomenon.

Picture this: The 90s and early 2000s. Gamers, previously islands in their own rights, began realizing there were other islands out there. Just over the horizon. Slowly, bridges were built. They weren't the high-speed, multi-lane superhighways we have now, but rickety dial-up connections, limited multiplayer modes, and forums hosted on the early versions of the World Wide Web.

Fast forward to today, and the numbers are staggering. As of 2021, there are over 3.1 billion gamers globally. That's nearly 40% of the world's population! From this massive number, over 1.5 billion are known to participate in some form of online multiplayer gaming. Compare this to the humble beginnings in the late 90s when being online often meant listening to the cacophony of dial-up tones, hoping the connection wouldn't drop. Those initial multiplayer forays numbered in the mere thousands, maybe tens of thousands if we're generous.

But what caused this shift? Why did a pastime, previously enjoyed in the warm glow of a single screen in a dimly lit room, suddenly explode into a kaleidoscope of shared experiences, international tournaments, and virtual friendships?

It's tempting to think that advancements in technology were the primary drivers. Faster internet speeds, more powerful gaming consoles, and sophisticated game designs undoubtedly played a part. However, at the core of this transformation was something more profound: an intrinsic human desire to connect, share, and belong.

This chapter delves deep into this evolution, this transition from gaming as a solitary endeavor to a bustling social hub. We'll explore the early days of multiplayer gaming, the birth of online communities, and how digital avatars became as significant, if not more so, than our real-world personas.

Join us on this journey, as we chart the course of gaming's metamorphosis from an individual hobby to a societal phenomenon. We'll discover how, in just a few decades, we've gone from the joy of a single-player campaign to the exhilaration of a global multiplayer arena. And in understanding this journey, perhaps we can gain insights into our own evolving nature in this ever-connected age. Welcome to Chapter 5: Gaming Gets Social.

# Multi-tap Multiplayer and Sleepover Game Nights

Ah, the multi-tap. It wasn't just a peripheral; it was a passport to another world. A world where four friends, instead of the usual two, could dive into the digital fray together. It transformed the solitary gaming experience, or the traditional two-player duel, into a social event. Suddenly, games weren't just about you, or even you and a friend. They were about the group, about collective joy, competition, and collaboration.

Remember those days? A pile of controllers tangled on the living room floor, the faint aroma of pizza rolls and popcorn in the air, and the muffled sounds of your favorite game's title screen echoing as a siren's call? These were the heralds of a sleepover game night.

It was the dawn of the Golden Age of couch co-op and competitive gaming. Sports games became raucous tournaments with brackets drawn on pizza boxes. Racing games were no longer about beating computer AI but out-maneuvering your best mate in the final lap. Even single-player games became a shared experience, with friends gathering around to watch, offer unsolicited advice, or impatiently wait for their turn after the inevitable "game over" screen.

These gatherings weren't just about gaming; they were about bonding. It was in these caffeine-fueled late-night sessions that friendships were forged in the fires of virtual battles. It was where alliances were tested in team games, and sometimes, where rivalries were born during particularly competitive matches. The playful jabs, the over-dramatic groans of defeat, the triumphant whoops of a last-minute win - these were the sounds that defined a generation.

Sleepover game nights also became a rite of passage. They were a domain where gaming etiquette was learned and where gaming folklore was passed down. Did your friend commit the cardinal sin of 'screen-peeking' during a heated 'GoldenEye' match? Or perhaps they chose the 'unbeatable' character in a fighting game, leading to endless debates and rematches.

However, beneath the surface of these jovial gatherings, something transformative was happening. Gaming was slowly evolving from being a mere hobby to a shared culture. Terms like 'camping', 'respawn', and 'co-op' became part of the vernacular. And it was during these sleepovers, these nights of shared passions and interests, that the foundation for today's massive online communities and eSports phenomena was laid.

To put it in modern terms, think of these gatherings as the beta version of today's MMOs. No, there wasn't an internet connection, and you couldn't team up with someone from another continent. But the spirit was the same. It was raw, it was genuine, and it was the beginning of gaming's journey from the fringes to the mainstream of social interaction.

The multi-tap was more than a device. It was a symbol of gaming's budding social nature. And while today's games have expanded the multiplayer concept to global proportions, there's still something inherently magical about those sleepover game nights of yesteryears. They were a testament to the power of gaming - not just as entertainment but as a medium that brings people together.

# The Rise and Fall of the Split-Screen

The split-screen. For many, this simple term is dripping with nostalgia. It evokes memories of crowding around tube televisions, squinting at one quadrant of the screen, and praying your sibling or friend wasn't sneaking a glance at your section. It was a time when the term "multiplayer" didn't mean online arenas or vast digital worlds but sharing half (or a quarter) of a television screen with your gaming companions.

In its heyday, split-screen gaming was a revolution. Games, inherently a digital experience, were given a very tangible, very human touch. You weren't playing against an anonymous avatar; you were playing against your brother, your best friend, or that cousin you only saw during the holidays. The competition was real and personal. Every victory was sweeter, and every defeat stung a bit more, especially with your opponent sitting right next to you, ready with a cheeky grin or a playful nudge.

Let's not forget the strategies that evolved specifically for split-screen play. Screen-peeking, the act of sneaking a look at another player's section of the screen, became the unsanctioned move everyone denied doing but occasionally indulged in. Arguments about screen-peeking became as much a part of the game as the game itself. "Were you looking at my screen?!" was a phrase yelled in living rooms more times than anyone could count.

However, with all its charm, split-screen gaming wasn't without its flaws. Screen real estate was a prized commodity. A game that looked magnificent in full screen could become cluttered and hard to navigate when split into sections. And for those who took their gaming seriously, distractions were everywhere. The peripheral movement from other sections, the ambient noise of your fellow gamers - it all added to the challenge.

Then came the inevitable shift. As the internet's tendrils began to spread, and technology made leaps, online multiplayer gaming began its ascent. Players weren't limited to inviting friends over; they could now connect with gamers across the globe. The world became the couch. This new era promised individual full screens, voice chat, and a level of immersion that split-screen couldn't compete with.

With this evolution, split-screen began its gradual decline. Game developers, eyeing the potential of online multiplayer, began to reduce their focus on local co-op modes. The allure of worldwide leaderboards, massive online tournaments, and the promise of endless new challenges from players around the world became the industry's new focus.

Here's a personal confession: There's something about split-screen gaming that remains unmatched. Yes, online gaming is fantastic. It has opened doors and created communities that were previously unthinkable. But split-screen had heart. There was an intimacy to it. A shared experience, not just in the game, but in the room. The high-fives after a victorious match, the shared bowl of chips, the collective groan after a close defeat. These tangible moments made gaming more than just an activity; it made it an event.

So, while the industry has moved on, and split-screen gaming is less prevalent, it'll forever hold a special place in the hearts of those who experienced it. It's a testament to the evolution of gaming. From shared screens to shared servers, the core desire remains the same: connection. Whether it's with the person beside you or a friend halfway across the globe, gaming's essence is about shared experiences.

In retrospect, split-screen might have been a stepping stone, a necessary phase before the digital explosion we see today. But oh, what a glorious stepping stone it was. The pixelated, chaotic, laughter-filled cornerstone of many a childhood. It remains a bittersweet chapter in the annals of gaming – a symbol of simpler times, when sharing a screen meant sharing memories.

# Friendships Forged and Tested in the Fires of Virtual Competition

In the realm of pixels and polygons, amidst the cacophony of explosive sound effects and the alluring glow of on-screen action, something profound was taking shape. Friendships, once determined by playground alliances or classroom seating arrangements, found a new incubator – the world of video games. This digital frontier became a place where bonds were both created and challenged, a space where camaraderie and competition blended seamlessly.

I remember, rather fondly, the first time I experienced the magnetic pull of this shared gaming experience. I was at a friend's house, a slightly awkward teenager with oversized glasses and a penchant for all things geeky. On that fateful evening, we decided to dive into a co-op campaign, a journey that promised both challenges and shared triumphs. As the hours blurred into a mix of strategy debates, mutual encouragements, and fits of laughter, I realized we were no longer just two friends hanging out; we were comrades-in-arms. The game wasn't merely a pastime—it was an experience, one that required teamwork, trust, and a bit of telepathic communication.

Speaking of telepathy, let's pivot to a funny anecdote. There was this one time during a particularly intense match, where my friend and I were convinced we had developed some sort of non-verbal communication superpower. At a pivotal moment, without uttering a word, we executed a perfectly synchronized in-game maneuver. Elation ensued, and we proclaimed ourselves gaming "mind-meld" champions. That is, until his younger sister pointed out that she had accidentally left her microphone on, broadcasting her team's strategy session directly to us. Our psychic prowess was debunked, but it became a cherished inside joke.

But it wasn't all smooth sailing. Gaming, with its fierce competitiveness and high stakes (virtual stakes, but stakes nonetheless), also became the litmus test for many friendships. The thrill of victory or the sting of defeat could amplify underlying tensions. I remember friendships that faced strains over 'unfair' tactics or 'cheap' game moves. On the battlefield of virtual competition, the lines between friendly banter and genuine frustration often blurred.

Yet, these trials by fire also had a flip side. They offered moments of reflection, opportunities for reconciliation, and lessons in sportsmanship and humility. It's one thing to lose against an anonymous online opponent; it's an entirely different emotional roller-coaster when you're bested by someone you'll see at school the next day. Learning to manage both the triumphant highs and the ego-bruising lows became an essential part of growing up in the gaming era.

And let's not forget the moments of sheer joy. Moments when the whole room would erupt in celebration after a hard-fought win or a particularly tricky level was finally conquered. There was something almost magical about those collective victories, where individual achievements took a back seat to shared success.

One personal realization I had during those years was how video games transcended traditional social barriers. The school's star athlete and the quiet bookworm could find common ground in the world of pixels. Shared gaming experiences became icebreakers, conversation starters, and bridges between seemingly disparate social circles. In that virtual realm, hierarchies faded, and genuine connections blossomed.

Looking back, it's clear that while the graphics, storylines, and mechanics of the games we played were important, it was the shared experiences that truly mattered. It was about those late-night gaming sessions that transitioned into deep conversations in the early hours of the morning. About the strategies planned, the challenges faced, the victories celebrated, and yes, the defeats mourned. Together.

In essence, video games became more than just a hobby or a pastime. They were a backdrop against which memories were crafted, friendships solidified, and life lessons inadvertently learned. Those digital landscapes, filled with challenges and adventures, became the arenas where many of us discovered aspects of our personalities, forged lifelong bonds, and, on occasion, found a bit of our own humanity reflected back at us.

# Chapter 6: Graphics, Graphics, Graphics!

Ah, graphics. That ever-important, always contentious, and eternally evolving realm of video gaming. You know, back in the day, two pixels bumping into each other was considered a major romantic subplot. Fast-forward a few years, and if a character's individual eyebrow hair isn't rendering in hyper-realistic 8K resolution, we're ready to revolt. But let's pump the brakes for a second and venture back to a simpler time.

Remember when the gaming world was divided not by console loyalty or preferred gameplay style, but by pixel count? Ah, the good ol' days when we'd squint at our screens, trying to determine if that blobby, eight-pixel mess was a space invader or just a particularly aggressive Tetris block. But as technology evolved and graphics started improving, so did our standards. And boy, did they skyrocket.

Now, I'm not implying that we became graphic snobs overnight, but let's be real; we did kind of turn into that wine connoisseur who insists on smelling the cork. We reveled in every graphical update, marveled at every new shading technique, and held long (and heated) debates over anti-aliasing, tessellation, and ray tracing, often without fully understanding what half of those words meant. The mantra became clear: Better graphics equalled a better game. Or did it?

The '90s and early 2000s were a fascinating era in this regard. As we transitioned from 2D to 3D, game developers seemed like kids in a candy store, experimenting wildly and offering us titles that ranged from visually breathtaking to... well, let's diplomatically call them "aesthetically unique". There were times when characters had hands that looked like shovels and heads that were suspiciously boxy. Ah, nostalgia!

But here's the irony. Despite our obsession with graphics, some of the most iconic games from this era were not necessarily the ones that pushed the graphical envelope. Sure, we loved the shiny and new, but a compelling story, innovative mechanics, and gameplay depth were equally captivating. Yet, every new console release or game announcement was (and still is) often met with that age-old question: "Yeah, but how are the graphics?"

We became a generation of pixel peepers, zooming into every screenshot, analyzing every shadow, and exclaiming, "Look at the realistic ripple of that pond!" or "Did you see the lifelike flutter of that NPC's cape in the background?" We'd cheer and applaud game trailers for their graphical prowess, sometimes overlooking clunky mechanics or half-baked storylines. It was a time when a game's success could hinge on its polygon count.

Yet, amidst this graphic-obsessed culture, there were poignant reminders of what truly makes a game special. Remember the first time you experienced a genuine emotional connection to a character, even if they were made up of clunky polygons? Or when a game's storyline left you in introspective silence, even if its world was more abstract art than lifelike representation?

In this chapter, we'll embark on a visual journey, charting the progression and obsession with graphics. We'll celebrate the milestones, chuckle at the missteps, and perhaps, just perhaps, remind ourselves that while graphics can dazzle and delight, it's the heart of the game that truly resonates.

So, ready your virtual cameras, sharpen those pixels, and let's dive deep into the world where every shade, shadow, and silhouette mattered. Welcome to the graphical rollercoaster of gaming's golden era!

# Pushing the Boundaries: Polygons, Pre-rendered Backgrounds, and Realism

Once upon a pixelated time, our game characters were flat. Not emotionally (well, maybe a little) – I mean two-dimensionally flat. It was an era where every action, jump, and movement was confined to a single plane. But as the '90s began to take shape, something remarkable was happening: games were shedding their 2D constraints and embracing the brave new world of 3D. Enter: polygons.

## The Polygon Revolution

When polygons entered the scene, they brought with them the promise of depth, shape, and a more immersive experience. Initially, these polygons were... how shall we put it? A tad on the rudimentary side. Characters often looked like they were constructed from a child's block set, and landscape elements bore a striking resemblance to origami. Remember Lara Croft's original triangular... assets? It was like the entire gaming universe had gone to geometry class, and the only thing they learned was the triangle.

Yet, despite their angular beginnings, polygons marked the start of a 3D revolution. The dream of creating lifelike characters and immersive worlds suddenly seemed achievable. Games began to incorporate complex models, detailed environments, and dynamic camera movements.

Think about the sprawling cities of "Grand Theft Auto" or the detailed dungeons of "The Legend of Zelda: Ocarina of Time." These worlds were detailed, expansive, and felt incredibly real, all thanks to the mighty polygon.

## Pre-rendered Backgrounds: A Brush of Artistry

In the quest for better graphics, developers employed another ace up their sleeves: pre-rendered backgrounds. By designing detailed, static backgrounds and overlaying 3D characters, games could achieve a look that was both artistically rich and visually stunning. This technique allowed for intricate details, moody atmospheres, and the illusion of depth without taxing the console's resources too heavily. Think about the haunting, ethereal streets of "Final Fantasy VII's" Midgar or the ominous mansion in "Resident Evil." These backgrounds set the tone and created atmospheres that simple 3D models couldn't achieve alone.

## Realism: It's All in the Details

With the building blocks of polygons and the artistry of pre-rendered backgrounds, games began to inch closer to the elusive goal of realism. Texture mapping draped our blocky characters in 'real' fabrics, dynamic lighting made in-game days transition to nights, and facial animations... well, let's just say they tried their best.

We started seeing water that reflected, shadows that moved with their sources, and hair – oh, the hair! – that fluttered with a will of its own. Games like "Silent Hill" used fog (partly to cover up rendering limitations) to create an ambiance of dread, while racing games showcased reflections on car surfaces, making them gleam under virtual sunsets.

Of course, realism came with its quirks. I remember one time, in a particularly gritty title, a character's hand went rogue and decided it wanted to exist outside the body. It floated around the screen, casting eerie shadows on the wall. Ah, the joys of early graphic realism! Those bugs were worth their weight in comedic gold.

In retrospect, this period was a visual playground. Developers were constantly pushing boundaries, experimenting with what was possible, and occasionally overstepping into the hilarious realm of the absurd. Yet, it was all in the name of progress, and what glorious progress it was. From flat planes to 3D worlds brimming with life and emotion, gaming was on a trajectory that promised even more wonders on the horizon. And as we smirked at the polygonal blunders, deep down, we were all wide-eyed at the marvel unfolding before us.

# Controversies Surrounding Violence and Realism – "Mom, it's just pixels!"

Ah, the sweet sound of controversy! Just as the gaming industry was stepping up its graphics game, there emerged a new breed of concerned critics. With games becoming more detailed and immersive, so too did the depictions of violence, gore, and other mature themes. Suddenly, our pixelated heroes weren't just jumping on mushroom-like creatures. They were involved in high-octane gunfights, edgy stealth assassinations, and fisticuffs that resulted in bone-crunching sound effects and splashes of vivid red. And the world took notice.

## Bloody Pixels Everywhere!

Remember the first time you saw blood spurt in a video game? It might have been in an arcade with "Mortal Kombat" or perhaps when the chainsaw revved in "Resident Evil 4." These games didn't just have violence; they flaunted it. Fatalities in "Mortal Kombat" were a spectacle, turning ordinary battles into gory performance art. Gamers were thrilled, but not everyone shared the sentiment.

## Public Outcry and the Dawn of Ratings

Headlines went berserk! "Video Games: Corrupting Our Youth?" screamed one tabloid. TV talk shows hosted animated debates, with one side arguing that these games were just harmless fun, while the other warned of a generation of desensitized psychopaths in the making. The concern reached such heights that it caught the attention of legislators. The U.S. Senate held hearings, and thus, the Entertainment Software Rating Board (ESRB) was born. Those familiar age and content ratings on game boxes? Thank the controversies of the '90s for that.

## Parental Woes and Late-Night Gaming Sessions

Every gamer of the era has a story. Mine? Sneaking into the living room for a late-night "Doom" session, only to be caught by my horrified mom as I chainsawed through a demon. "It's not real, Mom. Just pixels!" I tried to explain. But for her and many other parents, the line between digital violence and potential real-world consequences seemed perilously thin.

## A Debate Beyond Just Violence

The controversies weren't limited to just blood and gore. As graphics improved, games began to explore mature themes in more depth. Relationships, political intrigue, moral choices – suddenly, video games were growing up, and not everyone was ready for it. Games like "Grand Theft Auto" were celebrated for their open-world innovation but also criticized for their portrayal of women, crime, and a host of other issues.

## The Irony of It All

Here's the ironic bit. As much as the controversies raged, they played a pivotal role in shaping the gaming industry. They led to stricter regulations, true, but also to wider recognition. Video games weren't just child's play anymore; they were a force to be reckoned with, a cultural phenomenon that couldn't be ignored. The very debates that sought to limit the medium inadvertently gave it a broader platform.

In the pixelated dust that settled, one thing became clear: video games, with their polygons and pre-rendered backgrounds, had the power to evoke strong emotions, both in-game and out. They could make us cheer, cry, and even provoke societal debates. And as we gamers sat in our rooms, controllers in hand, rolling our eyes at the latest controversy, we knew we were part of something bigger, something transformative. Because, at the end of the day, they might be "just pixels," but oh, what a stir those pixels could create!

# From Pixel Art to "Is This a Movie or a Game?"

Once upon a time in the not-so-distant past, when you talked about video games, the first image that popped into most people's minds was Mario jumping over barrels, Space Invaders descending in pixelated monotony, or the unmistakable blip and beep of Pong. Fast forward to the late '90s and early 2000s, and you're not just playing a game – you're stepping into a cinematic universe, an interactive movie where every action or inaction, has consequences. But how did we make that leap from the rudimentary visuals of pixel art to the cinematic brilliance that had people second-guessing if they were holding a game controller or a movie remote?

## The Evolution of Game Graphics

By the time the PlayStation had established its dominance, developers were pushing the boundaries of what was possible in the realm of game graphics. Pixel art had its charm, no doubt. It was simple, efficient, and required players to use their imagination to fill in the gaps. However, as technology advanced, these tiny squares gave way to polygons, and the 2D side-scrolling worlds transformed into expansive 3D landscapes.

Titles like "Final Fantasy VIII" and "Metal Gear Solid" showcased what seemed like movie-quality cutscenes, blurring the lines between game and cinema. Environments were rich, characters showed actual facial expressions, and storylines were delivered with the gravitas of blockbuster films.

## Mainstream Media Takes Notice

This graphical renaissance didn't just stay confined to the gaming community. Mainstream media started taking notice. TV shows and movies began referencing video games not just as child's play, but as a form of art, a narrative medium that could stand toe to toe with Hollywood's best.

Perhaps the most significant nod from the entertainment industry came in the form of cinematic adaptations. Movies based on video games, like "Tomb Raider," starring none other than Angelina Jolie, found their way onto the silver screen. While not all were critically acclaimed, their mere existence spoke volumes about how far video games had come in the cultural zeitgeist.

## The Double-Edged Sword

However, with this newfound respect came a fresh set of challenges. As games became more cinematic, there was an increasing expectation for every title to have Hollywood-level storytelling, voice acting, and production values. This demand drove up development costs and times, putting pressure on studios to deliver hits consistently.

Moreover, some purists believed that in this drive towards cinematic perfection, games were losing their essence. They argued that while cutscenes and storylines were all well and good, games should prioritize gameplay. After all, if someone wanted to watch a movie, they'd go to the theater, not boot up a PlayStation.

## The Cultural Ripple Effect

Yet, there's no denying the broader cultural impact of this evolution. Video games began influencing other mediums. Movies adopted techniques from games, integrating first-person perspectives, or HUD-like visuals, reminiscent of the gaming experience. Music videos started emulating game graphics, and even fashion took cues from iconic game characters.

Conversely, the storytelling techniques from movies found their way into games, making narratives richer and more immersive. Characters weren't just avatars anymore; they had depth, backstory, and development arcs, further blurring the lines between gaming and cinema.

## In Retrospect

Looking back, it's evident that the evolution from pixel art to cinematic gaming was inevitable. The technology was there, the demand was there, and the artistic vision was there. And while we reminisce about the golden pixel days, there's no denying the magic of playing a game so visually and narratively compelling that you forget it's a game at all.

So, the next time you're engrossed in a beautifully crafted cutscene, lost in its narrative brilliance, and someone walks in asking, "Is this a movie or a game?" – take a moment to appreciate how far we've come and smile. Because, in a way, it's both.

# Chapter 7: Game Magazines & Early Internet Rumors

Ah, the '90s – when neon windbreakers were fashion staples, everyone wanted to "be like Mike," and the Spice Girls told us what they really, really wanted. But, amidst this iconic era, for the avid gamer, nothing spelled anticipation quite like the monthly game magazine drop or the first buzzings of rumors on the then-budding internet.

Before the immediacy of social media, before YouTube playthroughs and Twitch streams, there was the good old glossy game magazine. Players would eagerly await its arrival to dissect every screenshot, analyze each review, and, let's be honest, gaze longingly at those console ads that were still just outside our budget. These magazines were our bibles, our sneak peeks into upcoming titles, our guides to uncovering those oh-so-elusive Easter eggs.

And then there was the early internet – a digital wild west where one could stumble upon whispered rumors of secret levels, hidden characters, and cheat codes. Chat rooms became our secret meeting spots, and fan forums were birthed as sanctuaries for passionate discussions, speculations, and the occasional heated debate. The sense of community was palpable, and while the internet was still finding its feet, the gaming culture it fostered was alive and thriving.

This chapter dives into the nostalgic waters of gaming journalism's golden age and the dawn of the digital rumor mill. So, flip open those magazine pages in your mind, recall that unmistakable sound of dial-up connecting, and let's journey back to a time when game rumors were whispered in hushed tones and written word was king. Welcome to Chapter 7.

# Waiting Eagerly for the Monthly Magazine for Cheats, Reviews, and Demo Discs

Back in the '90s, if there was one thing that could rival the anticipation of an upcoming game release, it was the arrival of the monthly gaming magazine. In a world without instantaneous access to every trailer, gameplay footage, or gamer's review, these magazines were like the proverbial golden tickets into the chocolate factory of the gaming world.

## The Crinkling Sound of Fresh Print

You'd recognize it from the corner of your eye - the mail carrier rounding the bend, hopefully clutching that sacred parcel. Once in hand, the ritual would commence: the delicate removal of the plastic wrap, the first whiff of freshly printed pages, and the rapid flip through to find your favorite sections. Ah, the simple joys!

## Cheat Codes: The Precious Commodities

Before the days of easily accessible online walkthroughs and tutorials, cheat codes held an aura of mystique. They were the secrets whispered in school corridors, scribbled down in worn-out notebooks, or, more often than not, found in these monthly magazines. Unlocking a hidden character, bypassing

a challenging level, or accessing a secret area of the game –
these codes were more than just shortcuts; they were badges
of honor, earned through diligent reading or trading secrets
with friends.

## Reviews: The Make or Break

Trusting the opinion of internet strangers was still a distant
concept. In this era, a magazine's review held significant
weight. Gamers relied heavily on these analyses, using them
to make informed decisions about potential purchases or
trades. A highly recommended game would be talked about
for weeks, while a poor review would doom a game to the
dusty corners of video rental shops.

## Demo Discs: A Glimpse of the Future

Perhaps the most exhilarating part of the monthly magazine
package was the demo disc – a small, shiny circle of hope
and excitement. This disc allowed players to sample
upcoming games, diving headfirst into new worlds, if only for
a brief moment. For many, this was a chance to experience
titles they might never get to own, making these discs
treasured possessions.

In a way, these magazines were more than just publications;
they were monthly time capsules, capturing the evolving
zeitgeist of gaming culture. They built and nurtured a global
community of gamers, all eagerly awaiting that mail drop,

ready to plunge into a world of cheats, reviews, and tantalizing demos. The era might have been pre-digital in many ways, but the excitement, the passion, the fervor? That was as real as it gets.

# Urban Legends: Unlocking Lara Croft's Non-existent Nude Code and Finding the Triforce in Zelda

Ah, urban legends, the not-so-humble ancestors of today's clickbaity headlines. Before "You Won't Believe What Happened Next!" became a ubiquitous meme, there were whispers on playgrounds and in dimly lit arcades about the seemingly impossible feats within games. And boy, did we gamers bite into these tales, hook, line, and sinker!

## Lara Croft: From Ruins to Rumors

Let's start with the woman of the hour, the badass archaeologist with a penchant for somersaulting around traps and solving ancient riddles: Lara Croft. While her adventures in "Tomb Raider" captivated many, a rather mischievous rumor spread like wildfire – the existence of a cheat code that would, ahem, disrobe Ms. Croft. The irony? Lara, known for braving the deadliest of tombs in the swankiest of outfits, became the subject of gaming's most talked-about urban legend. And let's be real: the only thing being unveiled was our collective gullibility.

It's amusing to think that in a time when the 'Macarena' was a global dance phenomenon and Mulder and Scully were diving into extraterrestrial conspiracies on "The X-Files", gamers everywhere were covertly hitting button combos, hoping to stumble upon that elusive code. Alas, to the disappointment of many, the code turned out to be a cruel joke, and Lara continued her tomb raiding adventures in her usual attire.

## The Legend of Zelda: The Triforce Tease

Meanwhile, in the realm of Hyrule, another legend was brewing. "The Legend of Zelda: Ocarina of Time" promised gamers an epic quest, but an even more alluring mission emerged from the depths of gaming forums: the quest for the Triforce. An emblematic symbol in the Zelda series, the Triforce was curiously absent from Link's actual adventure in the game. Yet, rumors persisted that it was secretly tucked away somewhere, waiting for a worthy hero.

Countless were the hours spent by players bombarding every pixel of Hyrule, from the waterlogged depths of the Water Temple to the eerie halls of the Shadow Temple. There were "verified" methods floating around – certain songs to be played on the ocarina, specific sequences of defeating enemies, and even convoluted theories about talking to the right NPC at just the right time. Yet, the Triforce remained as elusive as the actual lyrics to "Lou Bega's Mambo No. 5".

## A Reflection on Our Gullible Selves

Why were these rumors so captivating? Perhaps they offered an additional layer of mystery in an age where games couldn't just update themselves with DLCs. Or maybe they were the gaming equivalent of trying to prove that if you played a certain '90s pop song backwards, you'd hear a message from aliens (looking at you, "Backstreet's Back" theorists).

The cultural zeitgeist of the '90s was rife with mysteries. Was Ross really on a break? How did the Fresh Prince's cab license plate say "Fresh" and have dice in the mirror? In the same vein, the gaming community had its own set of enigmas. And even though most of these legends were debunked, they added a layer of camaraderie among gamers, a shared experience of chasing the impossible.

In retrospect, these urban legends were a testament to the gaming community's passion, creativity, and, let's face it, sheer optimism. They were tales whispered between hushed breaths, hopeful secrets passed between eager fingers, and a delightful reminder of a time when not everything could be Googled away.

In the end, whether you were feverishly searching for Lara's non-code or embarking on Zelda's fool's errand, one thing was certain: these legends made the '90s gaming scene an epic quest of its own. And let's be real – weren't those fruitless endeavors, fueled by sheer hope and stubbornness, legendary in their own right?

# The Playground as the Original Game Forum

Oh man, just thinking about it takes me right back. Those were the days when 3 PM meant freedom, running out of those school doors and feeling the weight of academia lift for a few hours. The playground was our kingdom, and for a bunch of us, it wasn't just about the swings or the slides – it was the place where we convened to discuss the other realm we ruled: the world of video games.

You see, there's something raw and real about the memories of standing by the monkey bars, passionately discussing the latest game or sharing a secret cheat code. There was no Reddit, no Discord, no GameFAQs. It was just us, our experiences, and the wild rumors that flew faster than the school's gossip.

I remember when Johnny, with his unruly hair always sticking out from his cap, claimed he'd found a secret level in "Super Mario." Or when Sarah, who could do the best handstands, shared how she defeated a boss in "Final Fantasy." And of course, there was Alex, who'd always spin tales so wild about games that even the biggest gaming enthusiasts amongst us would raise an eyebrow in skepticism. Half the time, we could never tell if he was pulling our leg or if he'd genuinely stumbled upon some gaming gold.

But it wasn't just about the games or the legends. The playground was the place where we forged our earliest friendships over shared passions. It's where I met my best friend, Sam. We both were stuck at the same level in "Crash

Bandicoot," and after weeks of sharing tactics and strategies by the slides, we finally figured it out together during a sleepover. That victory felt more exhilarating than getting an A in Math (which, between you and me, was quite the rare occurrence).

The sheer joy of running to school the next day, knowing you've conquered a level or found a new secret passage, and sharing it with everyone – I miss that. Sure, today, we have the convenience of online forums, walkthroughs, and Let's Play videos. But there's something undeniably magical about those playground conversations, where our animated discussions painted vivid pictures even better than the best game graphics of our time.

Sometimes, late at night, when I'm navigating through a particularly tough level or exploring a new virtual world, I can't help but smile. Because I know that young kid inside me, the one who'd get overly excited about collecting all the stars in "Mario" or finding a hidden Easter egg, is still there. And every time I discover something cool in a game, there's a fleeting moment where I wish I could dash to the playground the next day and share it with everyone.

It's funny how something as simple as a school playground played such an integral role in shaping our love for gaming. In a way, those were our forums, our chat rooms, our community hubs. It was raw, it was real, and it was ours. And you know what? I wouldn't trade those memories for the world.

# Chapter 8: More Than Just Games

The beauty of video games extends far beyond the screen. It's more than just the pixels, the stories, the high scores, and the trophy achievements. As we sit here at the precipice of what feels like a new dawn in digital storytelling, it's essential to take a step back and appreciate how we arrived at this remarkable moment in history.

The rise of the video game industry has been nothing short of meteoric. But what is it about these games that resonates with millions, nay, billions, worldwide? Is it the escapism, the storytelling, the camaraderie, or perhaps something deeper? As we delve into the heart of how video games have transformed from a niche hobby into a defining element of millennial pop culture, we find that games have become a tapestry of our shared human experience.

## The Birth of a Behemoth: The Modern Game Industry

In the earliest days of video games, it was an experimental arena. These were small, pixelated endeavors, simple in design but rich in challenge. Fast forward through the arcade era, the first console wars, the rise of PC gaming, and the digital revolution, and we have an industry that rivals Hollywood in terms of revenue and influence.

Brands like PlayStation, Xbox, and Nintendo aren't just business entities; they're cultural touchstones. And as the hardware evolved, so did the software. Developers transitioned from creating games that were mere distractions to titles that are deeply engaging, emotionally resonant experiences. This evolution wasn't just about better graphics or more complicated mechanics. It was about narrative depth, character development, and a push to challenge the very idea of what a 'game' could be.

## A Reflection of Society: Games and Cultural Impact

As the industry blossomed, video games began reflecting and influencing society in a myriad of ways. They started addressing complex themes like mental health, politics, love, and loss. They allowed players to step into shoes they'd never wear in their real lives – be it a hero, a villain, a survivor, or even a god.

Games like "The Last of Us" delve deep into the human psyche, examining relationships and survival instincts, while titles like "Civilization" prompt players to consider the broader strokes of society and governance. These games, and countless others, use their platforms not just to entertain but to challenge, to question, and to inspire.

# The Beats of a Generation: Millennial Pop Culture

For the millennial generation, video games have become as defining as music was for the generations before. It's hard to separate the growth of this generation from the evolution of gaming. This is a generation that came of age alongside the rise of home consoles, the explosion of the internet, and the birth of mobile gaming.

Memes, fan fiction, fan art, and even fashion have been heavily influenced by video games. Consider the iconic, blocky look of Minecraft influencing design or the dance moves from Fortnite becoming viral sensations. Video games have become interwoven into the very fabric of millennial expression.

Furthermore, video games have broken barriers. We've seen the rise of eSports, where gamers aren't just players – they're celebrities, with fan bases rivaling those of traditional sports stars. The consumption of video game content, be it through Twitch streams or YouTube Let's Plays, highlights how games have become a spectacle, a shared event not just to play, but to watch, discuss, and celebrate.

In essence, video games have grown up alongside us. As we navigated the challenges of childhood, adolescence, and early adulthood, so too did our digital counterparts. They matured, broadened their horizons, and dared to dream bigger with each passing year. And as we move forward, one can't help but wonder: If this is where we've come in a few short decades, what incredible horizons await us in the future of gaming?

So, as we dive into this chapter, remember: This isn't just a tale of an industry. It's the story of a generation. It's the chronicle of how, in the face of adversity, criticism, and skepticism, video games emerged as a powerful, profound, and poignant force in the world of entertainment and beyond. This is the saga of how games became more than just games.

# Memory card woes: To delete or not to delete.

Ah, the memory card - that tiny, unassuming piece of plastic that held within it the power to bring both immense joy and heart-wrenching sorrow. In the world of ever-expanding digital content, where saving a game is as simple as a click and we measure storage in terabytes, it's almost quaint to remember the days when those few megabytes of storage space on a PlayStation memory card were the guardians of our virtual lives.

I recall one evening, a school night if memory serves, when I faced one of the most challenging decisions of my young gaming life. There it was, my beloved PlayStation blinking its saving icon, asking me a question I was woefully unprepared to answer: "Memory card full. Delete saved data to proceed?" I stared at the screen in disbelief. My Final Fantasy VII save file, with countless hours invested, sat alongside my progress in Crash Bandicoot, Metal Gear Solid, and many other cherished titles. Which one to sacrifice? It felt like being asked to choose between beloved pets.

And then there was "The Incident." My younger sister, in her innocent eagerness to start her own journey in Spyro the Dragon, had unknowingly deleted my near-complete Tomb Raider save. To say I was devastated would be an understatement. The magnificent mansion, the meticulously collected artifacts, and, most heartbreakingly, my progress through those treacherously tricky levels – all gone in an instant. A lesson was learned that day: always, ALWAYS, have a backup memory card (and maybe keep it hidden from mischievous younger siblings).

As trivial as these challenges may sound today, with our cloud saves and enormous hard drives, these moments shaped the experience of gaming in that era. The memory card wasn't just a storage device; it was a tangible representation of our achievements, our struggles, and the virtual worlds we'd come to cherish. Making the decision to delete a save was never just about freeing up space – it was about letting go of a piece of a world you'd invested so much in.

In those tiny blocks of saved data, we didn't just see game progress; we saw sleepless nights, hard-fought victories, and the companionship of characters we'd grown attached to. They were a testament to our dedication, perseverance, and the emotional investment we poured into these pixelated worlds. So, the next time you nonchalantly click 'save' on your latest game, spare a thought for those memory card pioneers, navigating the perilous seas of limited storage, and the heart-rending decisions they so often had to make.

# Customizing consoles: stickers, third-party controllers, and wild memory cards.

Ah, the late '90s and early 2000s, a time when self-expression wasn't just limited to questionable fashion choices and pop music; it extended right into our living rooms through the art of console customization. You thought those baggy jeans and frosted tips were a statement? Wait till you saw our PlayStation adorned with a galaxy of stickers.

First up, the stickers. Every console was a blank canvas, and every game, music album, or cereal box with a free sticker inside was the palette. From the proud display of a hard-earned achievement (remember those "I beat the game" stickers?) to the cringe-worthy pop star decals, we turned our consoles into a mosaic of our personalities, interests, and sometimes our breakfast preferences. I mean, who didn't want a cereal mascot right next to Lara Croft?

Then, there were the third-party controllers. Remember when your friend handed you that off-brand controller with the wonky joystick? Ah, the classic "Guest Controller," often deemed the "short straw" of gaming sessions. These off-brand monstrosities were sometimes twice the size of the official ones, with buttons that felt like they'd been borrowed from a toy phone. Yet, occasionally, amidst the sea of knock-offs, there was that one gem - the controller with the turbo button. Cheating? No! It was "strategic button pressing enhancement." Sure, it sounded like a jet engine taking off every time you used it, but boy, did it give you an edge in those button-mashing moments.

And let's not forget the wild memory cards. If the console was our canvas, the memory card was our... smaller canvas? From cards with little LCD screens that promised to display the game's logo (but usually just flashed a sad approximation of a pixelated blob) to ones with LED lights that could potentially double up as a landing strip for planes, the range was vast and often baffling. The grand promise of "double the storage" often resulted in half the reliability. But hey, it glowed in the dark, so who's complaining?

In essence, our customizations were a beautiful mess, a blend of personal flair, optimism, and, let's face it, some questionable design choices. But just like our teenage years, they were uniquely ours. And much like that butterfly sticker that's still stubbornly clinging to the corner of my old PlayStation, the memories stick too.

# The rise of game merchandise: posters, action figures, and everything in between.

Gaming in the late '90s and early 2000s wasn't just about basking in the glow of your CRT television, thumbing through cheat code magazines, or arguing about which console was superior. Oh no, it was an all-encompassing experience that spread its tentacles into every facet of our lives, turning our bedrooms into shrines dedicated to pixelated gods. Enter: the deluge of game merchandise.

Before the rise of PlayStation and its cohorts, your favorite game character might get, if they were lucky, a poorly made action figure or a basic T-shirt. But with gaming crashing into mainstream culture, suddenly Cloud Strife wasn't just a digital avatar; he was the brooding poster boy hanging on your wall, a miniature plastic figure striking a pose on your shelf, or even a keychain jingling in your pocket.

Posters were the quintessential teenage wall art. They were a proud proclamation of your gaming allegiances. A giant, looming poster of Final Fantasy's epic cast? Clearly, you were a sophisticated RPG enthusiast. A blazing, fiery backdrop with Crash Bandicoot's cheeky grin? Ah, an adrenaline junkie with a penchant for chaos. And these weren't just flimsy pieces of paper; they were battle flags, symbols of our tribes.

Action figures took on a life of their own. No longer confined to the likes of Star Wars or superheroes, gaming icons from Lara Croft to Solid Snake got the plastic treatment. These weren't mere toys. They were artifacts, intricate pieces of art that demanded to be displayed, not played with. God forbid someone actually tried to play with them! That's how arms got broken (the figure's, not the person's... mostly).

And then there was the miscellany, the unexpected, the strange. Alarm clocks that roused you with game theme tunes. Bedcovers that transformed your sleeping space into a pixelated dreamscape. Lunch boxes, school bags, pencil cases... if you could slap a game character on it, someone was selling it.

But amidst the sea of purchasable paraphernalia, the true magic was how these items transcended mere merchandise. They were extensions of our identities, badges of honor in a world that was just beginning to understand the cultural behemoth that gaming was becoming. These tangible tokens made the intangible world of pixels and code a concrete part of our reality. They let us literally hold onto pieces of these vast digital universes we loved and shared them with the world, one keychain, poster, or action figure at a time.

# Chapter 9: The World Outside PlayStation

Now, we've spent a great deal of time waxing poetic about PlayStation, dipping our toes into its sea of nostalgia, and reveling in the symphony of its iconic startup sound. But to think that the late '90s gaming universe revolved solely around Sony's shiny black box would be a gross oversight. It's like saying the '90s was only about frosted tips and baggy jeans. I mean, sure, they were undeniably present (and a crime against fashion), but there was so much more to the decade.

Enter the vast landscape outside the PlayStation realm. A land of pixelated wonders, offering experiences so varied and rich that even the most diehard PlayStation aficionado might be tempted to venture beyond their console comfort zone.

First stop: the PC gaming haven. Oh, the glorious world of LAN parties, where entire nights were consumed by StarCraft wars, and the morning sun wasn't a signal to sleep, but rather to launch another skirmish. The late '90s was when PC gaming went from being that weird cousin you only saw at family gatherings to the life of the party. We're talking about the birth of giants, my friends. Half-Life gave us a silent protagonist who spoke louder than words, and the world of Diablo ensured that clicking your mouse would never feel the same again. This was a time when graphics cards became a hot topic of discussion and when installing a game was an adventure in itself (remember those endless CD swaps?).

Meanwhile, in the realm of portable gaming, a storm was brewing. A storm, or should I say, a 'Pocket Monster' hurricane? The Pokemon fever was more contagious than any teen pop chartbuster. And the epicenter? The Game Boy Color. Remember trying to play it under the dim streetlights during late-night car rides? Or the convoluted trade setups to evolve that darn Machoke? It wasn't just a game; it was a phenomenon that changed the playground economy. Suddenly, your lunchbox trades were overshadowed by debates about whether Vaporeon was better than Jolteon.

And amidst this gaming renaissance, something even more significant was afoot. The tendrils of the gaming world began to weave their way into the very fabric of pop culture. Suddenly, Mario wasn't just a plumber leaping on Goombas; he was a symbol, an icon known even by your grandma who couldn't tell a joystick from a TV remote. Movies, music, fashion – gaming's mark was being stamped everywhere with a pixelated seal of approval.

So, as we dive into this chapter, strap in, dear reader. Leave your PlayStation bias at the door. We're stepping into a wider world, one where every corner of the screen holds a new surprise, where every beep and boop from a handheld could lead to a new adventure. It's a trip down the roads less traveled, but trust me, they make all the difference.

# PC Gaming: The Era of StarCraft, Half-Life, and Diablo

## A Revolution in Gameplay Mechanics and Storytelling

The late '90s weren't just the age of overalls and funky dance moves; it was also the time when PC gaming matured into an intricate tapestry of storytelling and mechanics. Let's break it down.

**Half-Life** wasn't just another first-person shooter. This game flipped the script on what players expected from the genre. Instead of the typical health packs and armor bonuses, players had to scavenge and use the environment strategically to survive. It brought a level of immersion we hadn't seen before, replacing cutscenes with a continuous narrative flow. Gordon Freeman, the silent physicist-turned-hero, became an embodiment of the player's actions, making us genuinely feel like a part of the chaotic Black Mesa Incident. There was no separation between player and protagonist, no cinematic breaks. Just pure, unfiltered immersion.

**StarCraft** redefined real-time strategy games in a manner no one saw coming. With its intricately balanced triad of races—Terran, Protoss, and Zerg—it wasn't just about who clicked the fastest, but who thought the quickest. Each faction had its strengths and vulnerabilities, demanding players to strategize and react in real-time. On a cultural level, in places like South Korea, StarCraft grew from a game to a full-blown sport, complete with pro-leagues, televised matches, and celebrity players. The game's intricate design made it as exciting to watch as it was to play.

**Diablo**, on the other hand, set the tone for action RPGs. Its isometric view, dark atmosphere, and a loot-driven system became staples for countless successors. But beyond the gameplay, Diablo proved that even in a hack-and-slash setting, a compelling narrative could thrive. The descent into the depths of Tristram, battling the hordes of Hell, became a journey of both character progression and unfolding lore.

## Graphical Evolution and Aesthetics

As technology advanced, so did the visual fidelity of PC games. The '90s witnessed a significant leap in this department. Games transitioned from simple 2D sprites to complex 3D models, and our PC monitors bloomed with previously unseen colors and details.

StarCraft, with its detailed units and sprawling maps, showcased how strategy games could be both complex and beautiful. Each unit, from the nimble Zergling to the towering Battlecruiser, was a work of pixel art, brimming with intricate animations and character.

Half-Life and Diablo, by contrast, demonstrated the leaps and bounds made in creating 3D environments. Their worlds felt lived-in, every corner filled with details, every shadow hiding potential threats. It's hard to forget the eerie green glow of radioactive waste in Black Mesa or the chilling Gothic architecture of Diablo's dungeons.

## The Social Aspect and Communities

The dawn of the internet era brought gamers from across the globe onto a singular platform. This connectivity transformed PC gaming from a solitary activity into a thriving social phenomenon.

Bulletin Board Systems (BBS) and later, forums became the gathering spots for players. Strategies were dissected, stories shared, and friendships forged. StarCraft's Battle.net became a landmark, connecting players in real-time, facilitating multiplayer matches, and creating a sense of global community.

Mods and custom content flourished, especially around Half-Life. The game's mod-friendly architecture gave birth to titles like Counter-Strike, which would go on to shape multiplayer gaming for decades. Communities rallied around these mods, providing feedback, building custom levels, and even creating entirely new narratives.

## Cultural Impact and Legacy

Each of these titles left an indelible mark on the gaming landscape. Their design principles, storytelling methods, and community-driven content have influenced countless titles that followed.

The significance of StarCraft in esports cannot be overstated. It laid the groundwork for competitive gaming, proving that with the right balance and design, a game could captivate audiences both playing and watching. Meanwhile, Half-Life's storytelling techniques have become a standard in narrative-driven games, emphasizing immersion and player agency.

Diablo's dark, atmospheric design, coupled with its loot-driven gameplay, has been echoed in numerous titles, from the Dark Souls series to the Destiny franchise.

Reflecting on the late '90s PC gaming era, it's clear that it wasn't just a period of technological advancements; it was a renaissance of creativity and innovation. To those of us who lived through it, there was an unmistakable energy, a sense of being on the cusp of something transformative.

The burgeoning PC gaming realm of the late '90s wasn't just about polygons, resolutions, or refresh rates, even though these technical facets had their undeniable allure. It was about the breaking of previous limitations, not just in terms of technology, but also in narrative depth, gameplay mechanics, and social connectivity.

Remember the first time you set foot in the sprawling Black Mesa facility in Half-Life? Or the chills that ran down your spine as the haunting Tristram theme played in Diablo? These weren't just games; they were experiences, meticulously crafted digital worlds that felt as real and palpable as our own. They raised the question: could a game make us feel genuine fear, elation, or despair? The answer was a resounding yes. We weren't just players; we became inhabitants of these worlds, emotionally invested in every challenge, plot twist, and character.

But these games did more than just tell stories or offer engaging gameplay mechanics. They challenged the status quo. They posed questions about what gaming could be and should be. They set precedents, becoming the benchmarks for all future titles in their respective genres. Games became more than just distractions or pastimes—they became platforms for storytelling on par with movies or literature.

During late-night gaming sessions, as I battled Zerg rushes or traversed the Lambda Complex, I remember pausing to marvel at the intricate details of these virtual worlds. They were testaments to the passion and dedication of their developers. Each game felt like a labor of love, reflecting the soul and creativity of its creators.

The innovations of this era laid the foundational stones for the gaming industry's future. Games began to be recognized not just as entertainment but as art forms, with the power to communicate complex ideas, elicit profound emotions, and comment on society and humanity. They became cultural phenomena, crossing boundaries and bridging gaps between people from all walks of life. They spawned communities, fan theories, fan arts, and modding cultures, solidifying the idea that games were collaborative experiences, shaped as much by their players as their creators.

Looking back, what strikes me most is the audacity of these games. In an industry that can often play it safe, sticking to tried-and-true formulas, these titles dared to dream. They took risks, whether in terms of gameplay design, narrative choices, or technical innovations. And more often than not, their gambles paid off, giving us some of the most memorable gaming experiences of our lives.

Today, as the gaming industry continues to evolve, it's crucial to remember and honor this golden era. For it was during this period that gaming truly found its voice, breaking free from the shackles of convention and soaring to new, previously unimaginable heights. And as someone who was fortunate enough to witness and be a part of this evolution firsthand, I can't help but feel a profound sense of gratitude and nostalgia. The late '90s wasn't just an era of games—it was an era of dreams, aspirations, and, above all, unbridled passion.

# Portable Gaming: Pokemon Hysteria and the Game Boy Color

## Introduction to Portable Gaming:

In the spectrum of gaming history, there are few moments as revolutionary as the birth of portable gaming. When we think back to the late 80s and 90s, it's not just the home consoles that grab our nostalgia-tinted glasses; it's the memories of sneaking in a quick game under the desk, during a school break or on a long car trip, clutching that trusty, somewhat chunky device. The introduction of Nintendo's Game Boy marked not just a milestone for the company, but for the very fabric of gaming culture.

The original Game Boy, released in 1989, was a gray, brick-like contraption. With its monochromatic greenish screen and humble specs, by today's standards, it may seem a tad underwhelming. But, back in its prime, this device was nothing short of groundbreaking. It brought beloved titles like Tetris, Super Mario Land, and The Legend of Zelda: Link's Awakening directly into our pockets. Gone were the days when gaming was tethered solely to the living room TV; the Game Boy allowed players the freedom to game anywhere and everywhere.

As the years progressed, so did the technology. Enter the Game Boy Color in 1998, a successor that managed to build on the legacy of its predecessor in every imaginable way. It was sleeker, more ergonomically designed, and as the name suggests, it introduced a vivid color palette to the handheld gaming experience. Games were no longer just shades of green and black; they were vibrant, dynamic, and even more immersive.

The Game Boy Color's launch saw a plethora of titles designed to exploit its color capabilities. However, no discussion about the Game Boy Color can commence without mentioning its crown jewel – Pokemon. But, more on that later.

The shift from the original Game Boy to the Game Boy Color wasn't just a leap in technology; it was emblematic of the evolution of gaming itself. Players now had expectations. They wanted richer narratives, better graphics, and more intricate gameplay mechanics, even in a device that could fit snugly in a pocket.

The rise in popularity of portable gaming was meteoric. The Game Boy Color sold millions, cementing its place as one of the most successful handheld gaming devices of its time. It wasn't just the device; it was the culture around it. Children discussing their latest catches in Pokemon during recess, swapping game cartridges, and the sheer excitement of unwrapping a new game and popping it into the back of the device – these are memories shared by countless millennials around the world.

In essence, the transition from the Game Boy to the Game Boy Color wasn't just a technological evolution; it was a cultural shift. Gaming was no longer an activity restricted to one's home; it was an on-the-go experience, something personal yet shared, a testament to how far we've come in the vast, diverse world of video gaming.

## The Pokemon Phenomenon:

In the late '90s, a craze swept the globe, infiltrating schoolyards, living rooms, and conversations. The phrase "Gotta Catch 'Em All!" wasn't just a catchy slogan; it was a clarion call to millions. That's right – we're diving headfirst into the cultural tidal wave that was Pokemon.

The inception of this global phenomenon began with the introduction of Pokemon Red and Blue (or Green for our friends in Japan). Released for the Game Boy, these games dropped players into a world filled with mystical creatures, challenging them to become the ultimate Pokemon Trainer. It wasn't just about battles or gym badges; the true allure lay in the Pokedex, a digital encyclopedia of Pokemon. With 151 unique creatures scattered across the Kanto region, players were bitten by the bug (or Bug-type Pokemon) of collecting.

Each Pokemon had its personality, its quirks. From the fiery charm of Charizard to the electric appeal of Pikachu, players developed genuine attachments to their pocket monsters. And then there were the tales of the elusive, rare Pokemon – whispers about a Psychic-type creature named Mew, hidden and waiting for a lucky trainer.

The genius of Pokemon Red and Blue wasn't just in its gameplay; it was in its design. Two versions, each with exclusive Pokemon, encouraging trade between players. It was a masterstroke. Suddenly, the playground wasn't just for hopscotch or tag. It became a bustling Pokemon market, with link cables connecting Game Boys as players bartered for that one Pokemon missing from their collection.

The 'collect-them-all' craze was real and all-consuming. Completing the Pokedex became a badge of honor, a bragging right. Friends became rivals, rivals became allies, all in the pursuit of the elusive title of Pokemon Master. Players would spend hours upon hours, grinding, searching, and trading, all to hear that sweet melody indicating a complete Pokedex.

But beyond the game mechanics, Pokemon tapped into a universal human urge – the desire to explore, to collect, to achieve a sense of completeness. It wasn't just a game; it was a journey. And for many, it was a shared experience, one of camaraderie, competition, and sheer joy.

In essence, Pokemon Red and Blue didn't just introduce a game. They birthed a phenomenon, a culture that transcended age, geography, and language. A culture that, decades later, still resonates with millions worldwide.

## Cultural Impact: The Pokemon Legacy Beyond the Game Cartridge

When we think of global cultural phenomena from the '90s, a few key things might spring to mind: The unmistakable riffs of grunge music, the angsty charm of teen dramas, or the eclectic fashion trends. Yet, there's one phenomenon that not only captured the zeitgeist of the era but has continued to evolve and thrive for decades – Pokemon.

Beyond the pixels of the Game Boy screen, the world of Pokemon rapidly expanded into various mediums, taking root in the collective imagination of a generation.

## Spin-offs, Merchandising, and the Pokemon TV Series:

Before long, Pikachu wasn't just a digital entity you battled with. He was everywhere. Stuffed toys, lunchboxes, t-shirts, and hats. There was a tangible world of Pokemon merchandise. And it was BIG.

Then came the spin-offs – trading card games that added a tangible, tactile element to the Pokemon experience. Kids everywhere were not just trading Pokemon in their games but swapping holographic Charizards and Ancient Mew cards in school playgrounds, local hobby shops, and at dedicated Pokemon League events. These cards became currency, some more coveted than others, leading to intense negotiations and the occasional playground skirmish.

And if that wasn't enough, the Pokemon TV series burst onto screens. Ash Ketchum (or Satoshi, named after Pokemon's creator, Satoshi Tajiri) and his trusty Pikachu set off on their adventure. With the iconic theme song, "I want to be the very best," we were hooked. Week after week, we tuned in to follow

Ash's journey, his challenges, the Pokemon he encountered, and the friends he made along the way. Characters like Brock and Misty weren't just sidekicks; they were our friends. The TV show made the Pokemon world even more tangible, offering narratives and stories that went beyond the game.

## How Pokemon and Portable Gaming Permeated Mainstream Culture:

Pokemon became more than just a game or a TV show. It became a cultural staple. The franchise permeated mainstream culture in surprising ways. Hollywood celebrities were spotted wearing Pokemon gear. Major news outlets covered the 'Pokemon phenomenon'. It was a legitimate craze.

This Pokemon phenomenon coincided with the era of portable gaming gaining mainstream acceptance. The Game Boy, with its portability and communal gaming experiences, democratized gaming. It wasn't just something you did alone in your room. It was something you shared with friends, siblings, and even parents.

The portability of the Game Boy and the collaborative nature of Pokemon (think trading and battles) transformed gaming into a more social pastime. It changed perceptions. Suddenly, gaming wasn't just for the 'hardcore gamers'; it was for everyone. This shift was monumental.

## Schoolyard Trades, Discussions, and Communal Gaming:

Let me take you back to a time when, at the ripe age of 9, the school bell's ring for recess was the starting bell for something else – a flurry of Pokemon activity. I remember unzipping my backpack, pulling out my trusty Game Boy, and joining a huddle of friends. We'd compare Pokedexes, set up trades, or just discuss the latest episode of the TV show. Those 15 minutes of break felt like a glorious hour in the Pokemon world.

It wasn't just about who had the rarest Pokemon or the most gym badges. It was about sharing strategies, discussing which Pokemon types were best for certain battles, and predicting where Ash's journey would take him next on the TV show. Even if someone didn't have a Game Boy or wasn't into the game, they were still part of the conversation. They might've collected the cards or simply loved the show.

Those playground sessions were more than just gaming breaks. They were our first forays into a community, a shared universe of like-minded enthusiasts. In that shared experience, friendships were forged. We learned about negotiation (that trade where I finally got a Bulbasaur was a masterclass in diplomacy), about competition, and about camaraderie.

In essence, Pokemon, through its multiple mediums – the games, the cards, the TV show – did something quite special. It brought people together. It turned gaming from a solitary activity into a communal experience. And in doing so, it changed the cultural landscape, setting the foundation for how we perceive and engage with games today.

# Gaming's Entry into Mainstream Media

From the dark, musky arcades to the shining screen of your living room TV, the journey of video games has been nothing short of a meteoric rise. Once perceived as a digital distraction for children and a refuge for socially awkward teens, video games have steadily asserted themselves as one of the dominant pillars of the 21st-century entertainment industry. But how did we transition from those quirky "pong" noises to narratives so deeply embedded in our cultural psyche? Let's rewind the tape and embark on a pixelated pilgrimage back in time.

Picture this: It's the early '80s. The disco era has taken its final bow, and rock and roll is on the rise. Amidst the neon lights and cassette tapes, a revolution brews not in grand arenas but in small, dimly lit rooms filled with bulky machines. Arcade halls. They're noisy, packed, and electric with anticipation. From schoolkids to office goers sneaking a break, everyone is huddled around screens, their eyes glazed over with concentration, fingers rapidly tapping on joystick buttons. Gaming was more than just a fad; it was a burgeoning subculture.

Movies and television, the two titans of popular media at the time, couldn't help but notice. Here was a phenomenon drawing crowds like bees to honey. Films began integrating arcade motifs and gaming narratives. Who could forget the iconic 1982 movie "Tron"? A film where characters were literally sucked into an arcade game, it was the wildest fantasy of every gamer come true on the big screen. Not only did "Tron" showcase a virtual world formed of game elements, but it also highlighted the escalating craze around video gaming. But that was just the beginning.

The 1983's "WarGames" pushed the narrative further, flirting with the terrifying idea of a computer game nearly causing World War III. A young Matthew Broderick using a video game interface to unintentionally threaten global annihilation was both alarming and oddly captivating. The underlying message? The power of video games transcended beyond mere entertainment; it could influence, for better or worse, the real world.

Television wasn't far behind in this digital embrace. By the mid-80s, cartoons featuring video game characters like "Pac-Man" and "Super Mario Bros." began to air. Children were not just playing games in arcades; they were now watching their favorite game characters come to life every Saturday morning, battling foes and going on adventures.

In essence, the 1980s saw a pivotal shift in video games from being just another pastime to becoming an essential part of the cultural narrative. It was no longer a niche; gaming started shaping the broader entertainment spectrum. Arcades might have been the petri dish where the gaming culture initially grew, but it was the nod of acknowledgment from films and television that cemented its place in mainstream culture. Gaming was not only here to stay; it was set to conquer.

Fast forward to today, and the lines between video gaming and pop culture have not just blurred; they've intertwined in a dance so intricate that it's hard to tell where one ends and the other begins. But to truly appreciate the nuances of this union, one must look back at the era when quarters clinked into machines, high scores were the currency of bragging rights, and gaming found its first allies in the cinematic and televised realms. The arcade may have been the cradle, but it was the embrace of mainstream media that propelled gaming into its golden age.

## Pop Culture Icons Born from Gaming

In a world swamped with media, where movie stars and music icons traditionally reigned supreme, a new breed of celebrities began to emerge in the latter part of the 20th century. They weren't born in Hollywood studios or under the bright lights of Broadway. Instead, they came to life in code, pixels, and polygons, challenging every preconceived notion of fame and stardom. Enter the era of video game icons.

Let's start with a plumber. Not just any plumber, mind you, but one clad in red, sporting a mustache that's become iconic, and a penchant for saving princesses. Mario, of the eponymous "Super Mario" franchise, didn't just leap over Goombas; he made a vault into our collective consciousness. Children wanted to be him, adults found him oddly relatable, and everyone, irrespective of age, hummed the legendary background score as they went about their daily lives. But what truly skyrocketed Mario into pop culture immortality was his leap from the console to the big screen and TV. Though the 1993 "Super Mario Bros." film adaptation may not have been a blockbuster hit, it signaled a monumental moment:

video game characters had cultural currency powerful enough to warrant Hollywood's attention.

Now, on the other end of the spectrum, racing against the backdrop of green hills and collecting rings, was Sonic the Hedgehog. This blue, spiky speedster not only gave SEGA its mascot but also a seat at the table of cultural icons. Sonic's attitude, his rebellious streak, epitomized the 90s' counter-culture spirit. He wasn't just a character; he was a statement. TV shows, comics, and a slew of merchandise later, Sonic's prominence in pop culture was undeniable. And while not every adaptation did justice to our beloved hedgehog (looking at you, initial CGI design for 2020's "Sonic the Hedgehog" film), his significance remained undiminished.

But not all gaming icons were cute or cartoonish. Emerging from the 3D-rendered depths of ancient tombs and dense jungles came the formidable and fierce Lara Croft. "Tomb Raider" wasn't just a game; it was a revolution. Lara, with her twin pistols, athletic prowess, and a sharp intellect, shattered the glass ceiling for female protagonists in the gaming world. She was neither a damsel in distress nor a side character; she was the hero. Lara's rise to fame culminated in her portrayal by none other than Angelina Jolie in two big-budget film adaptations. The very fact that an A-list Hollywood actress donned the mantle of a video game character was testament enough to gaming's pervasive influence.

Master Chief, the faceless protagonist of the "Halo" series, stands as an emblematic figure of gaming's 21st-century surge. Enigmatic and clad in green armor, he resonated with an audience that was grappling with a post-9/11 world. While Master Chief might not have made the same cinematic waves as his fellow icons, his sheer omnipresence, from memes to merchandise, echoed a sentiment: You didn't need a face to become a pop culture behemoth.

While we cherish the successful forays of these characters into cinema, it's essential to acknowledge the missteps. Let's not forget the cringe-worthy "Super Mario Bros." film or the convoluted "Assassin's Creed" movie. But even in their failures, they illuminated a salient point - adapting video game narratives into traditional formats was no easy task. Yet, their mere existence proved that gaming had not just entered the pop culture arena; it was now a formidable contender.

In essence, the 90s and early 2000s witnessed an unprecedented shift. Characters born from keystrokes and coding became as recognizable, if not more, as many silver screen stalwarts. They inspired Halloween costumes, were the subjects of schoolyard debates, and graced the covers of magazines. The pixelated underdogs of the entertainment realm had truly had their Cinderella moment, and the world, mesmerized, watched on, game controller in hand and popcorn at the ready.

## The Music of Gaming

The haunting strings of the "Halo" theme, the simple yet unforgettable tune of "Super Mario Bros.," the melancholic piano notes from "Final Fantasy" – these are but a few anthems that resonate with generations of gamers. To outsiders, they might be nothing more than background noise, a mere supporting act to the pixels dancing on the screen.

Yet, to those who've held a joystick or pressed a keyboard in earnest, these soundtracks are the pulse of countless digital adventures, the unsung heroes of the gaming realm.

Imagine, for a moment, Mario without his upbeat, catchy theme or "The Legend of Zelda" sans its stirring melodies. These games would lose an integral part of their charm and identity. The music is not just an accessory; it's the soul, the essence that transforms a collection of coded interactions into a rich, immersive experience. It's no coincidence that the chirpy tunes from Tetris get stuck in our heads or that the ethereal notes from "Journey" move some to tears. These compositions play with our emotions, setting the mood, and often acting as our only companion during solitary in-game expeditions.

In the early days of arcade games, music was elementary, often consisting of monotonous beeps and boops. However, the constraints of 8-bit technology didn't deter composers from creating magic. Koji Kondo, while working on the "Super Mario Bros." theme, for instance, didn't have the luxury of a full orchestra or the latest synthesizers. Yet, with limited resources, he crafted a tune so iconic, so universally recognized, that it can easily stand alongside some of the greatest pop hits of its era. Fast-forward a few years, and this once-humble background track could be heard in schoolyards, ringtones, remixes, and even on the lips of those who had never held a game controller.

In the realm of role-playing games, especially the "Final Fantasy" series, the music played a pivotal role in storytelling. Tracks like "To Zanarkand" or "Aerith's Theme" didn't just accompany a scene; they amplified the narrative's emotions.

Composer Nobuo Uematsu didn't merely create a soundtrack; he wove a rich tapestry of feelings, seamlessly blending them with the on-screen drama.

But as video game music evolved, it didn't just remain confined to the gaming world. It started permeating mainstream culture. The soundtracks began to gain recognition not just as background game music but as genuine pieces of art. Marty O'Donnell's compositions for "Halo" are a testament to this. The haunting monk chants, combined with stirring orchestral movements, were so impactful that they birthed a new phenomenon: video game music concerts. Fans would flock to venues, not for pop stars or classic rock bands, but to hear their favorite in-game anthems performed live. The "Halo" suite, played by a full orchestra, sent shivers down the spines of listeners, reiterating the power and depth these compositions held.

Parallel to this, game soundtracks started getting noticed at major music award functions, with some even bagging prestigious accolades. It was a significant acknowledgment – a nod from the traditional music industry, recognizing video game music's depth, complexity, and artistry.

And then came a phenomenon that no one anticipated – games where music was the protagonist. Titles like "Guitar Hero" and "Dance Dance Revolution" transformed living rooms into stages, making gamers the stars of their rock concerts and dance parties. These games underscored music's universal appeal, uniting both gamers and non-gamers in rhythmic harmony.

As video games began to resemble cinematic experiences, the line between film and game soundtracks blurred. Renowned composers, traditionally linked with Hollywood, began lending their talents to the gaming industry. Hans Zimmer's work on the "Call of Duty" series is a shining example. The bombastic, adrenaline-pumping tracks brought the same intensity to the game as they did to blockbuster films.

In retrospection, video game music's journey reflects the broader trajectory of the gaming industry. From humble, pixelated beginnings to grand, cinematic masterpieces, the evolution has been nothing short of spectacular. These soundtracks have given voice to silent protagonists, evoked tears in the most stoic of gamers, and energized countless multiplayer battles.

To say that music in video games is just an accompaniment would be a gross understatement. It's the heartbeat, the silent companion, the unsung hero. Whether you're a plumber hopping across mushroom-filled kingdoms, a soldier in an intergalactic war, or a wanderer in a post-apocalyptic wasteland, the music ensures you never truly journey alone.

## Art, Literature, and Theater: Gaming's Unanticipated Legacy

It's a strange and beautifully chaotic world we're living in when Pac-Man rubs pixelated shoulders with Picasso, when Lara Croft's escapades inspire Broadway numbers, and when a gamer's fanfiction rivals the intensity of Dostoevsky's best works. The classical realms of art, literature, and theater, once guarded by purists and gatekeepers, have seen a digital invasion—a storm of ones and zeroes, pixels and polygons—that has left an indelible mark on modern culture. Here's the irony: the traditional world of aesthetics, which once sneered at video games, is now borrowing, imitating, and, dare I say, evolving, thanks to them.

Let's delve deep, shall we?

## Pixel Palette: The Gaming Canvas in Art Galleries

Art, in its essence, is a reflection of the times. So, it's no surprise that the rise of gaming has birthed an entirely new school of thought in the art world. Consider the scenario: dimly lit rooms in renowned art galleries, once reserved for Rembrandts and Van Goghs, now feature Mario jumping across screens or the neon glow of "Tetris" blocks. Digital art and pixel art exhibitions are becoming increasingly mainstream, and for a good reason. They represent a unique blend of nostalgia and futurism—a harmony between the analog and digital realms.

Pixel art, in particular, has become an emblem of this movement. What was once a technical limitation of early gaming systems has now evolved into a full-fledged artistic style. Artists use chunky, square pixels to portray scenes that range from the comically absurd to the profoundly melancholic. There's a certain purity, a rawness, to these pixels, untainted by the realism of today's graphics. They're a testament to the idea that constraints often breed creativity.

But it's not just pixel art that's making waves. Game design itself, with its intricate level layouts, character designs, and environmental aesthetics, is being dissected and celebrated. Exhibitions delve deep into the creative processes behind iconic games, showcasing early sketches, storyboards, and prototypes. To walk through these galleries is to journey through the evolution of gaming, witnessing its growth from rudimentary Pong paddles to the hyper-realistic worlds of today.

## Literary Levels: When Gaming Inspires Books

Literature and video games, at first glance, might appear poles apart—one steeped in centuries of tradition, the other a relatively new kid on the block. Yet, the gaming universe, bursting at its digital seams with rich narratives and complex characters, has become a goldmine for authors.

Remember when "Ready Player One" exploded onto the literary scene? Ernest Cline's ode to gaming and '80s pop culture wasn't just a novel; it was an experience—a nostalgic trip down memory lane for gamers and a cultural excavation for newcomers. The book's success underscored a pivotal shift: gaming was no longer just a pastime; it had seeped into our collective literary consciousness.

Moreover, fanfiction platforms are teeming with tales spun from gaming universes. These aren't just amateur scribbles; they're passionate, intense narratives that expand and sometimes even rival the source material. These stories underscore the power of games to inspire, to give birth to whole new worlds, characters, and sagas.

## All The World's A Game: Gaming Takes Center Stage

The world of theater is no stranger to adaptations. From Shakespearean plays reimagined in modern settings to books brought to life on stage, the theater has always been a melting pot of ideas. Enter video games—a medium ripe for theatrical exploration.

Imagine the iconic scene from "Final Fantasy VII" where Cloud Strife mourns Aerith, portrayed on stage, the heart-wrenching music echoing through the auditorium, and the audience, a mix of gamers and theater-goers, collectively holding their breath. This is the potential of gaming in theater. The rich tapestries of game narratives, combined with the immediacy of live performances, can create magic.

There are now plays and musicals inspired by gaming culture. They dissect the gamer psyche, explore the blurred lines between virtual and reality, and celebrate the communal spirit of gaming. These aren't mere adaptations; they're evolutions, taking the essence of a game and molding it into something new, something profound.

In conclusion, the influence of gaming on art, literature, and theater isn't just about pixels on canvases, stories on pages, or characters on stages. It's about a cultural shift, a redefinition of boundaries. It's about recognizing that video games, once dismissed as child's play, are now shaping, influencing, and enriching our most treasured forms of expression. The joystick, it appears, is mightier than the pen, brush, and stage spotlight combined. And as we level up into an era where gaming's influence is omnipresent, one can't help but be excited for the next level of this incredible journey.

## The Impact of Gaming Lingo: Power-Ups in Everyday Conversation

It's a Friday evening, and you're at a cafe with a friend. As you recount your workweek, you mention how you managed to "level up" at your job, earning a promotion. Your friend, listening intently, nods in understanding, shooting back with their own tale of narrowly avoiding a "game over" situation with a project deadline. Both of you chuckle, sharing a silent nod to the gaming culture that has inadvertently shaped your conversation. But when did "respawning" from a challenging week or seeking to "unlock achievements" in real life become part of our daily vernacular?

# The Integration of Gaming Terminology

From the early days of arcade cabinets flashing "Insert Coin" to the multiplayer lobbies of today where players discuss strategy before "respawning" in a match, gaming jargon has experienced a fascinating evolution. These terms, once confined to the virtual realms of 8-bit landscapes, have seamlessly transitioned into our daily conversations, so much so that even those unfamiliar with gaming can understand their broader connotations.

The term "level up" serves as an apt example. In games, it signifies growth, progress, and the enhancement of abilities. In real life, we use it to depict personal or professional advancement, a testament to our accomplishments. Similarly, "respawn" might evoke memories of coming back to life in a first-person shooter game, but it's also become synonymous with bouncing back from setbacks or starting afresh.

This crossover isn't mere coincidence. It reflects a cultural acceptance and acknowledgment of gaming's influence on society. As games became more complex and narratives richer, their language became more nuanced, allowing for broader applications in real-world contexts.

# Cultural Implications of Gaming Language

The adoption of gaming lingo into everyday speech has several broader implications. Firstly, it underscores the universality of the gaming experience. As these terms become commonplace, it suggests a shared understanding, a collective experience that transcends age, nationality, and background. Gaming, once a niche hobby, is now a global phenomenon, and its language reflects this shift.

Moreover, this transition of terms from the screen to real-life conversation signifies the erasure of boundaries between the "gamer" identity and the general populace. As gaming went mainstream, so did its vocabulary. Parents, teachers, professionals, and kids all "power up" their mornings with coffee, face "boss battles" in their daily tasks, and occasionally need to "reboot" their systems after a taxing day.

Furthermore, the infusion of gaming terms in everyday language showcases the medium's power to influence and shape societal norms. Just as literature, cinema, and music have contributed to the linguistic tapestry, gaming, too, has stitched its colorful threads into the fabric of conversation. These terms, laden with meaning and memories, enrich dialogues, offering new ways to express age-old sentiments.

In conclusion, as gaming continues to burgeon, establishing itself as a prominent pillar of modern culture, its lexicon will likely further embed itself in our daily interactions. These words, once mere indications of progress or failure on a screen, now resonate with emotions, aspirations, and experiences. They're not just terms; they're narratives, stories of pixels and people intertwined in a dance of evolution. So, the next time someone says they're trying to "unlock achievements" in life, smile knowingly, for the game of life, much like its virtual counterparts, is filled with challenges, power-ups, and endless opportunities to "level up."

# Cultural Crossovers: Games Meeting Traditional Media

Roll credits! No, wait... Press start? Ah, the lines have blurred.

Once upon a time, in a not-so-distant past, movies and video games occupied separate realms in the vast entertainment galaxy. Movies, with their larger-than-life visuals and heart-wrenching performances, were reserved for the grand theaters, while video games, pixelated adventures, and digital tournaments, found solace in the buzzing arcades and living rooms. But, as Bob Dylan so aptly crooned, "The times they are a-changin'."

## From Reels to Joysticks and Back Again

Enter the era of crossovers, where the silver screen met the digital screen in a dazzling dance of adaptation. This isn't just about movies getting game adaptations or games getting cinematic treatments; it's a tale of two mediums finding mutual respect, understanding, and immense potential in each other's arms.

Let's rewind. Remember rushing to the arcade or booting up your console to play games based on your favorite movies? 'Jurassic Park,' 'Die Hard,' and yes, even the 'Street Fighter' games, which would later make their way back to the screen in, let's just say, interesting ways. These game adaptations, although varying in quality, were clear evidence of the gaming world's reverence for film.

But what happens when the relationship is reversed? In recent years, we've witnessed games, with their rich worlds and intricate stories, becoming compelling fodder for filmmakers. The 'Assassin's Creed' movie tried to capture the heart-stopping parkour and historical tapestries of its game counterpart. While its success is debatable, its existence points to a trend: games are no longer mere child's play; they're epic narratives worthy of Hollywood's attention.

## The Peak of Adaptation: The Witcher's Roaring Success

If one had to pinpoint a beacon of success in game-to-show adaptations, it would be hard to overlook Netflix's 'The Witcher.' While technically based on Andrzej Sapkowski's book series, there's no denying that the game series catapulted Geralt of Rivia into global stardom. The show, with its catchy bard tunes and complex characters, resonated with both gamers and non-gamers alike. It's a testament to what happens when an adaptation respects its source material, understanding the core of its appeal.

## A Journey Fraught with Challenges

However, this path of adaptation isn't always paved with gold coins and XP points. For every 'The Witcher' series, there's a

'Super Mario Bros.' movie, which, although nostalgic for some, is often remembered with a mix of confusion and amused disbelief. The challenge lies in translation. Games are interactive, personal, and sprawling. Movies and shows, by contrast, follow a linear narrative, with limited runtimes and a more passive engagement from the audience. Striking a balance, ensuring that the essence of a game is captured while crafting a coherent cinematic experience, is no easy feat.

## Conclusion: A Love Story for the Modern Era

As we stand at the crossroads of culture, watching as movies and games continue their delicate waltz, it's evident that these two mediums, although distinct, share a core essence. They're both about storytelling, immersion, and evoking emotions. Whether you're clutching a controller, guiding a character through a treacherous quest, or sitting in a dimly lit theater, eyes glued to the screen, you're embarking on a journey. It's a journey of adventure, laughter, tears, and awe. And as these worlds continue to collide and collaborate, one can only wait with bated breath, popcorn (or game controller) in hand, eager to see what the next level of this relationship holds.

# Gaming's Influence on Technology and Design

At a glance, the arcades of the '80s and the sleek smartphones of today may seem worlds apart. Yet, they share a common DNA, a legacy of gaming that has, over the decades, reshaped the technological landscape and deeply impacted design aesthetics across various platforms.

## Pushing Boundaries: Gaming's Need for Speed and Power

Gaming has always been about pushing boundaries. The race to render more polygons, to animate more lifelike characters, and to immerse players in increasingly realistic environments has driven advancements in hardware like perhaps no other industry. Gamers, in their relentless pursuit of better experiences, became an audience forever hungry for more power, faster speeds, and greater fidelity.

Consider the graphic card wars between giants like NVIDIA and ATI (now part of AMD). Each year, they'd unveil new GPUs, promising richer visuals, higher frame rates, and more immersive experiences. This wasn't just a competition; it was a race to meet the ever-evolving demands of the gaming industry. These advancements didn't just benefit gamers. Video editors, 3D artists, and other professionals reaped the rewards, enjoying faster rendering times and smoother workflows.

# A Revolution in Interface Design

When we think of gaming's influence on design, it's not just about the neon hues of a cyberpunk cityscape or the 8-bit nostalgia of indie games. Gaming has, in more ways than one, reshaped how we interact with devices. The intuitive nature of modern touchscreens, the ergonomic design of controllers, and even the rise of virtual and augmented reality owe a debt to gaming.

Take, for example, the Nintendo Wii. Its motion-controlled gameplay was revolutionary, offering a novel and physically engaging way to interact with games. This innovation laid the groundwork for advancements in gesture recognition technology, which is now commonplace in many non-gaming applications.

## The Aesthetics of Playfulness

As games became an integral part of our cultural fabric, their distinct aesthetic began to seep into other areas of design. The playful icons, vibrant color palettes, and interactive animations that were once the domain of gaming started appearing in software interfaces, mobile apps, and even websites.

Consider the "gamification" trend, where apps, from fitness trackers to learning platforms, adopt game-like reward systems to engage users. The badges, progress bars, and achievement unlocks feel eerily similar to leveling up in a game.

Then there are design elements that echo the gaming world. The neon glows, pixel art, and digital motifs that you find in many modern apps owe their inspiration to the vibrant and imaginative world of video games.

## Conclusion: A Synergy of Play and Progress

In essence, the world of gaming has not only entertained us but has also been a relentless force propelling technological innovation and influencing design aesthetics. Its impact isn't just seen in the beefy gaming rigs or the latest VR headsets but in the very fabric of our digital interactions. From the smartphone in your pocket to the interactive kiosk at a museum, the footprints of gaming are everywhere, reminding us that at the heart of innovation often lies the simple joy of play.

# Conclusion: The Cultural Feedback Loop

As the curtain falls on our exploration of gaming's intertwining saga with popular culture, we find ourselves standing at the cusp of a new dawn. A dawn where digital landscapes and real-world narratives aren't two distinct entities but a melded tapestry of experiences, influences, and shared memories. We've journeyed through the pixelated alleys of the '80s, surfed the roaring waves of the '90s, and now, in the neon-lit boulevards of the 21st century, the story of gaming and pop culture is written in bold, dynamic strokes on every billboard.

## Cultural Confluence: An Eternal Dance

Games are not born in a vacuum. They are a reflection, sometimes a reaction, to the world around them. Similarly, pop culture isn't a static domain. It pulses, breathes, and evolves, absorbing elements that resonate with the zeitgeist. Herein lies the magic: while games draw inspiration from pop culture, they simultaneously contribute to it, creating a feedback loop of influence that's both intricate and profound.

Consider the '80s, an era of glam rock, space fantasies, and an infatuation with the future. Video games of the time, like "Space Invaders" and "Asteroids," were very much a product of this fascination. Fast forward to the new millennium, and we find games like "Mass Effect" and "Dead Space" not only drawing from space operas like Star Wars but also adding their own rich lore to the genre.

## From Pixels to Reality: The Cycle Continues

The rise of virtual and augmented reality is further blurring the lines. Games are no longer confined to screens; they're leaping into our living rooms, streets, and social spaces. The phenomenon of Pokémon GO, where digital creatures inhabited real-world locales, was just the beginning. As AR and VR become increasingly sophisticated, the delineation between game and reality will become even more nebulous.

The implications are profound. Will future art installations not just be something to observe, but something to 'play'? Could our favorite TV series in the future be interactive VR experiences where we walk alongside our favorite characters, influence plots, or even change outcomes?

## The Future: An Evolving Tapestry

Looking forward, the gaming industry isn't just set to influence pop culture; it's poised to be an indomitable pillar of it. With the rise of esports, gaming celebrities are becoming just as influential as film or music stars. Game soundtracks are not just background noise; they're chart-topping hits. And game narratives aren't secondary tales; they're epic sagas discussed and dissected with the fervor reserved for classic literature.

Yet, with great power comes great responsibility. As gaming's voice grows louder in the cultural choir, there will be challenges. Issues of representation, inclusivity, and the potential for over-commercialization will come to the forefront. But if history is any indication, the gaming community is resilient, adaptive, and innovative.

## In the Mirror of Time

As we peer into the shimmering horizon of the future, it's evident that the tale of gaming and pop culture is one of mutual growth and evolution. It's a dance where each partner takes the lead at different times, guiding the other into new terrains and experiences.

The feedback loop between gaming and pop culture has created a dynamic ecosystem. One where stories, characters, and experiences flow seamlessly between mediums, enriching each other. It's a world where a book can inspire a game, which inspires a movie, which inspires a song, which inspires...another game.

## Epilogue: A Universe Unfolding

In this grand odyssey, we've unearthed treasures of insight, marveled at the intricate interplay of gaming and pop culture, and envisioned a future that promises even richer confluences. The joystick and the cinema reel, the VR headset and the novel, the pixel and the paintbrush – they're all threads in a vast, vibrant tapestry of human expression.

So, as we set our controllers down, let's not see it as the end but a pause. A brief respite before the next level, the next chapter, the next verse in this unending, exhilarating saga of play, passion, and pop culture. The game, dear reader, is far from over.

# Chapter 10: Pioneering the Digital Frontier

The transition from the 20th to the 21st century was not just marked by the tick of a clock but by a tidal wave of technological advancements. As we sailed into this new era, the gaming industry, ever the forward-thinker, began laying the groundwork for a revolution. A revolution that would reshape the very fabric of how we played, interacted, and experienced gaming. This chapter takes us on a journey through that crucial period of transition, tracing the early seeds of modern gaming and setting the stage for the explosive growth that was to come.

In retrospect, the late 1990s and early 2000s can be viewed as a time of experimentation and exploration. Game developers and hardware manufacturers alike began testing the waters of what was possible with emerging technologies. The world was quickly moving online, and the gaming community wasn't about to be left behind. The introduction of the Dreamcast's modem, for instance, hinted at the tantalizing possibilities of connecting gamers across continents, laying the early foundations for what would later become a booming online multiplayer universe. The notion that a player in Tokyo could race against someone in New York or collaborate with a team in London was no longer the stuff of science fiction; it was becoming reality.

Yet, it wasn't just about connecting gamers; it was about enriching the gaming experience itself. The rise of MMORPGs

(Massively Multiplayer Online Role-Playing Games) offered players not just games but worlds. Worlds that were vast, persistent, and ever-evolving, where thousands of players could craft their narratives, forge alliances, or even engage in epic battles. These weren't just games; they were living, breathing digital realms that mimicked the complexities of our real world.

Parallel to this was the evolution of the gaming console. No longer were these devices merely platforms to play games. They were evolving into multimedia hubs. With the introduction of features like DVD playback, suddenly, the humble gaming console was competing for prime real estate in the living room, not just the bedroom of a teenager. It symbolized the broader acceptance and integration of gaming into mainstream entertainment.

And then there was the anticipation, the palpable excitement in the air, as whispers grew about a new player entering the arena. Sony's PlayStation 2 was on the horizon, and with it came promises of groundbreaking graphics, immersive experiences, and a new chapter for gamers worldwide. A chapter that would solidify gaming's place not just as a hobby but as a central pillar of pop culture.

In this chapter, we'll delve deep into these transformative years. We'll explore the challenges faced, the successes celebrated, and the lessons learned. More importantly, we'll witness the industry's relentless drive to innovate, to push boundaries, and to chart new territories. For while the games themselves were evolving, so too was the very idea of what gaming could be. This was a period of setting precedents, of planting the seeds that would grow into the mammoth industry we recognize today.

So, as we journey through this crucial era, let us appreciate the visionaries, the risk-takers, and the dreamers who saw not just where gaming was, but where it could go. For in their ambition and determination, they didn't just set the stage for the future; they built it. Welcome to Chapter 10.

# Seeds of Online Gaming: The Dreamcast's Modem and Early MMORPGs

The dawn of the new millennium carried with it more than just the hope of a fresh start. It bore the whispers of a new era in gaming—an era where the boundaries of play would extend beyond the walls of our living rooms, reaching out to touch distant shores and unfamiliar lands. There's a palpable nostalgia when one thinks back to this era, not just for the games themselves but for the sense of wonder they inspired.

The Sega Dreamcast, a console that often found itself overshadowed by its heavyweight competitors, was the unsuspecting harbinger of this digital revolution. Many remember the Dreamcast for its intriguing game library or its unfortunate premature exit from the market. However, in the annals of gaming history, its most crucial contribution was perhaps its built-in modem. This wasn't just a feature; it was a statement, an assertion that the future of gaming was online.

The magic wasn't just in the modem's existence but in the possibilities it unlocked. Gamers, for the first time, had a taste of what it was like to race against opponents from across the globe in real-time, to embark on co-op adventures with friends from other continents. The Dreamcast's modem was a portal, a gateway that gave us a fleeting glimpse into a connected gaming universe.

Parallel to this was the emergence of MMORPGs on the PC. These were no ordinary games; they were sprawling digital realms that lived and breathed. Games like 'EverQuest' became more than mere pastimes; they were alternate lives lived in virtual worlds. The very idea that one could embark on grand quests, form guilds, engage in trade, or even just sit by a digital campfire and chat with fellow adventurers from all over the world was nothing short of revolutionary.

It's easy to look back at those early MMORPGs with a sense of fondness, remembering the pixelated graphics, the clunky user interfaces, and the painfully slow internet speeds. Yet, the heart of these games wasn't in their technical prowess but in their ability to forge genuine human connections. Gamers made friends, rivals, and sometimes even found love. They celebrated in-game weddings, mourned the passing of legendary guild leaders, and debated lore with the fervor of scholars.

But perhaps the most poignant nostalgia lies in the innocence of it all. The novelty of online interaction, the thrill of hearing a voice from the other side of the globe, and the sheer joy of collaborating with strangers who became friends. This was a time before microtransactions, before the debate over loot boxes, and long before online toxicity became a mainstream concern. It was pure, unadulterated joy. It was the Wild West of online gaming, uncharted, untamed, and brimming with possibilities.

In retrospect, the Dreamcast's modem and the rise of early MMORPGs were not just products of their time but visionaries of the future. They sowed the seeds for a connected world, a world where gaming was not just about reflexes or strategy but about community, camaraderie, and shared experiences. As we journey through this section, let's not just remember the games or the technology but the emotions they evoked, the bridges they built, and the world they promised—a world we are fortunate to inhabit today.

# Consoles as Multimedia Devices: DVDs and Beyond

In the annals of gaming history, there's a definitive moment where consoles began to break their shackles, evolving from mere gaming machines into full-fledged entertainment hubs. The catalyst? The advent of the DVD.

As the 90s drew to a close, Sony made a bold move with the PlayStation 2, introducing not just a gaming console but an all-in-one entertainment system. The PS2, sleek in design and robust in capabilities, came equipped with a DVD player. This was monumental. For many households, the PS2 became the primary DVD player, a bridge between the worlds of gaming and cinema. You could switch from racing in "Gran Turismo" to watching "The Matrix" without ever swapping the device connected to your TV.

But Sony's integration of the DVD player was more than just an added feature—it was a statement. A declaration that consoles were no longer just for the gaming niche but aimed squarely at the heart of mainstream entertainment. The ramifications of this move were profound. It set a precedent, heralding a future where consoles would be judged not just by their gaming prowess but by their multimedia capabilities.

The DVD's inclusion opened up a new frontier for game developers too. With its vast storage capacity compared to the previous generation's CDs, developers now had the space to craft larger, more intricate game worlds, weave denser narratives, and include full-motion video sequences that rivaled Hollywood productions.

Post-PS2, the trajectory was set. Successor consoles like the Xbox 360 incorporated HD-DVD drives, the PS3 flaunted a Blu-ray player, and before we knew it, consoles were streaming Netflix, playing music, and even browsing the web.

In retrospect, the integration of DVDs into gaming consoles was a pivotal point. It transformed our perception, morphing consoles from playthings of the dedicated gamer to central entertainment hubs in living rooms worldwide. The lines between gaming, film, and television began to blur, paving the way for the immersive, multifaceted entertainment ecosystems we enjoy today.

# Anticipating the PlayStation 2 and the Next Chapter of Gaming

As the dawn of the new millennium approached, the world of gaming stood on the precipice of an evolution, one that would redefine the very fabric of the industry. At the heart of this transformation was an emblem of anticipation, a symbol of the future: Sony's PlayStation 2.

Even before its release, the PlayStation 2 was the stuff of legends. Whispers of its capabilities spread like wildfire through the gaming community. Would it truly be the multimedia powerhouse it was touted to be? Could it merge the world of gaming with other entertainment forms seamlessly? The answers would soon become evident, but the anticipation itself was palpable.

Sony had already made waves with its original PlayStation. Its library, teeming with iconic titles, had set a gold standard. But with the PS2, Sony wasn't just aiming to set a standard; it sought to revolutionize. A built-in DVD player, backward compatibility, and an intricate design made the console a coveted piece of tech from the get-go. But it wasn't just about the hardware; it was the promise of experiences yet to come.

The games that would grace the PS2 in its lifespan have since become the stuff of legend: "Shadow of the Colossus," with its atmospheric storytelling and giant foes; "Grand Theft Auto: San Andreas," which gave players an entire state to explore and disrupt; and "Final Fantasy X," pushing the envelope on narrative depth and graphical prowess. These titles were merely the tip of an iceberg that promised and delivered unparalleled gaming experiences.

This anticipation, this promise of the future, was more than just about better graphics or innovative gameplay. It was symbolic of a gaming industry coming of age, ready to stand toe-to-toe with established entertainment mediums. Gaming was no longer the domain of the few; it was now a cultural phenomenon. The PlayStation 2 was set to be not just a console but a conduit to a new era.

In many ways, the PS2 was the herald of modern gaming. It pushed boundaries, both in terms of what a console could do and what games could achieve narratively and emotionally. The anticipation surrounding its release was a testament to a community ready and eager for change, for evolution. And as the PS2 soared to become the best-selling console of all time, it was clear: the next chapter of gaming had begun, and it was glorious.

The PS2 era set the stage for what was to come—more immersive games, more powerful consoles, and a gaming culture that would permeate every corner of global entertainment. But for those who stood in line, eagerly waiting for their PS2 all those years ago, it was about being part of a moment, a movement. It was about being on the cusp of something monumental, anticipating the future of an industry they loved.

# Conclusion: A Legacy in Pixels

The echoes of history often reverberate in the most unexpected of places. In the realm of gaming, those echoes take the form of pixels, fragments of memory, and the digital footprints of a bygone era. The period spanning from 1994 to 2001 wasn't just a chapter in gaming's storied journey; it was a transformative epoch, a seismic shift that catapulted video games from niche corners to the epicenter of global entertainment.

Few could have predicted the monumental impact that a gray box from Sony would have on the cultural zeitgeist. The PlayStation, and its subsequent iteration, was more than just a gaming console. It was a symbol of change, of progression. It was the dawn of a new era where stories told through polygons and pixels became as powerful and resonant as those told through words or on film reels.

And as we stand today, on the threshold of hyper-realistic virtual realities and augmented worlds, we can trace the roots of our advancements back to this pivotal time. The digital landscapes we traverse, the avatars we embody, the worlds we inhabit—all bear the indelible mark of that transformative era. The foundations laid during those seven years continue to shape and influence the contours of modern gaming, from indie titles to blockbuster franchises.

In this concluding exploration, we'll journey back to those formative years, diving deep into the enduring legacy they've carved. We'll dissect the influence of that iconic gray box, contemplate its reshaping of entertainment, and cast our gaze forward, into the shimmering horizons of what's yet to come in the realm of virtual reality, augmented reality, and beyond. So, buckle up, dear reader, as we embark on a final ride through the pixels and passions that have defined a generation.

# The Enduring Influence of the 1994-2001 Era on Modern Gaming

Ah, the years between 1994 and 2001 – when plaid shirts were all the rage, dial-up modems reigned supreme, and a pixelated Italian plumber could become an overnight superstar. This era was a pivotal chapter in gaming, not just because it introduced us to some of the most legendary titles, but because it sowed the seeds for modern gaming's forest of innovation.

Let's kick things off with the **3D Graphics Revolution**. Gone were the flat, 2-dimensional avatars that we maneuvered around the screen. The gaming world erupted into three-dimensional splendor, pushing us headfirst into unfamiliar terrains. The leap from 2D to 3D wasn't just a visual one; it was a leap of faith, marking the first step towards today's virtual and augmented realities. The blocky but aspirational 3D models of Lara Croft and Cloud Strife are now immortalized as the vanguards of this shift, icons that beckoned gamers into vivid, sprawling universes.

This era wasn't just about polygons and graphics; it redefined **Storytelling Evolution**. The '90s might have been the era of cheesy sitcoms on TV, but in the world of gaming, stories took a deep, introspective turn. Games began to narrate tales that mirrored blockbuster films, with plots brimming with twists, turns, and cliffhangers. From the soulful journey of a flower girl in the sprawling city of Midgar to the tragic tale of a bandicoot twisted by science, games became more than just play – they became experiences. They taught us about love, betrayal, friendship, and the gray shades in between.

Speaking of gray shades, the gaming content of this period matured faster than a teen left home alone for the first time. The **Content Maturation** of this era was palpable. Gone were the days when games catered solely to the whims of children. With titles like 'Silent Hill' and 'Resident Evil,' players were thrust into dark, intense, and sometimes psychological narratives, making it clear that gaming was not just child's play anymore.

This was also the time for **Genre Expansion**. No longer were players confined to the strict corridors of platformers or simple beat-em-ups. This era saw the genesis of every conceivable genre, from mind-bending puzzles to sprawling strategy epics. You wanted to be a lawyer in a world full of quirky characters? There was a game for that. How about a sim where you play God and control every aspect of your characters' life? Yep, there was a game for that too.

One thing's for sure, the '90s knew how to socialize, and the **Birth of Gaming Communities** was testament to that. Gaming began to transcend boundaries, connecting players worldwide. From the early seeds of multiplayer showdowns in 'GoldenEye 007' to the vast online realms of 'EverQuest,' a sense of community began to flourish. Gamers weren't just isolated enthusiasts anymore; they became part of vast, interconnecting networks, laying the foundation for today's massive MMOs and eSports scenes.

Let's not forget the unsung heroes of this period - the **Technological Innovations**. Who could forget the excitement of buying a larger memory card or the anticipation of loading a game from a CD-ROM? These might seem trivial today, but back then, they were groundbreaking, pushing the gaming experience to uncharted territories.

And how can we discuss this era without touching on its role in popular culture? Gaming icons began rubbing shoulders with film stars and musicians. Gaming in Mainstream Culture saw Mario breaking onto the big screen (albeit with dubious success), while titles like 'Final Fantasy' received full-fledged film adaptations. Video games were no longer the preserve of the bedroom; they were shining on the red carpet.

In essence, the period from 1994 to 2001 wasn't just a golden age for gaming – it was the crucible from which modern gaming was forged. The lessons, the innovations, and the experiences of that time continue to ripple through today's industry, shaping our experiences and setting the stage for the future. And while we now play in vast, hyper-realistic worlds, let's not forget the pixelated roots from which we sprung.

# How a Gray Box from Sony Reshaped Entertainment

In the annals of gaming history, few moments are as transformative as the debut of Sony's gray behemoth, the PlayStation. Sure, it was just a gray box – but to dismiss it as such would be akin to labeling the Mona Lisa as "just another portrait." The PlayStation wasn't just a game console; it was a cultural juggernaut, a revolution in a box that would forever change how we view and engage with digital entertainment.

Before its entrance, the gaming landscape was predominantly dominated by Nintendo and Sega, the Goliaths of the industry. These giants had a solid grip on the market with their family-friendly mascots and fast-paced platformers. And here came Sony, the proverbial David, aiming to shake the pillars of this established world. But rather than a sling and stone, Sony's weapon of choice was the PlayStation, an unassuming gray box that packed a wallop.

At its core, the PlayStation's primary advantage was its **Technological Prowess**. While cartridges limited the scope of narratives and graphics in games, Sony's adoption of CD-ROMs was groundbreaking. This provided game developers with a massive playground to craft intricate narratives, cinematic cut-scenes, and expansive game worlds. 'Final Fantasy VII,' with its sprawling discs, was a testament to this newfound freedom. It told stories in a manner that was, until that point, confined to the domain of Hollywood.

Sony wasn't just selling a console; they were marketing a **Lifestyle Choice**. The PlayStation became a symbol of cool. Its sleek design, its edgy commercials, and its vast library appealed not just to kids, but to teenagers and adults as well. With titles like 'Metal Gear Solid' and 'Silent Hill,' Sony was clear in its message: Gaming isn't just for kids; it's a mature, sophisticated form of entertainment.

This maturity extended beyond game titles. Sony actively courted third-party developers, leading to a Diversified Gaming Library that catered to all tastes. Want a heart-pounding racer? 'Gran Turismo' had you covered. Craving a horror-filled jaunt through a foggy town? 'Silent Hill' awaited. This eclectic mix ensured that every gamer, irrespective of age or preference, found something to resonate with.

The PlayStation also brought with it a sense of Community and Connectedness. Memory cards allowed players to share game saves, leading to increased social interactions. The MultiTap accessory let four players compete or cooperate, making gaming a group activity. The conversations around games, strategies, and hidden easter eggs transformed the PlayStation from a solitary pastime to a shared experience.

But the PlayStation's influence extended beyond the gaming realm. It impacted Mainstream Media and Popular Culture. The console's success propelled gaming into the spotlight, making it a staple in popular culture. Characters from PlayStation titles became household names, merchandise flooded stores, and game soundtracks found their way onto CD shelves and music players.

To sum it up, that gray box from Sony was more than just a piece of hardware; it was a paradigm shift. The PlayStation blurred the lines between gaming and cinematic storytelling, between child's play and adult entertainment, and between niche pastime and cultural phenomenon. It wasn't just about reshaping the gaming industry; it was about redefining entertainment in the digital age. The echoes of Sony's gray box reverberate even today, a testament to its indelible mark on the world of entertainment.

# A Nod to Today: VR, AR, and Where We're Headed

In our journey through the halcyon days of the PlayStation era, we've navigated the pixelated pathways and marveled at the polygonal progress that has led us to the gaming horizon of today. The 1994-2001 era was undeniably transformative, setting the stage for the leaps and bounds that would come in the ensuing decades. Yet, as we stand on the precipice of this new age, we're confronted with gaming realities that seem to have jumped straight out of the pages of sci-fi novels: Virtual Reality (VR) and Augmented Reality (AR).

**Virtual Reality** has taken us by storm, thrusting gamers into immersive worlds where they are no longer mere spectators but active participants in the narrative. The visceral experience of VR is unparalleled, allowing us to soar through alien skies, battle dragons up close, or simply live an alternate life. It's an evolution that the early pioneers of gaming could only dream of. Games like 'Beat Saber' and 'Half-Life: Alyx' are pushing the envelope of what's possible, making us rethink the very foundations of gameplay and interaction.

But while VR offers immersion, Augmented Reality provides integration. AR cleverly melds the digital with the real, overlaying our world with a layer of virtual wonder. The success of 'Pokémon GO' was a testament to AR's potential, turning our mundane surroundings into arenas of fantastical capture battles. Through AR, our living rooms can become racetracks, our backyards can morph into battlefields, and our cities can transform into massive multiplayer arenas.

Yet, for all their wonder, both VR and AR are still in their infancy, much like how the original PlayStation was in its early days. There are challenges to overcome, from technical limitations to the very human issues of motion sickness and disorientation. But, just as the gray box from Sony broke barriers and redefined expectations, so too will VR and AR. They're not just the next step in gaming; they are the next leap in how we experience stories, engage with art, and interact with one another.

This cyclical nature of gaming's evolution, from the humble origins of Pong to the hyper-realistic realms of VR, reminds us that we're part of an ever-evolving narrative. The games we play, the stories we cherish, and the experiences we share are all chapters in this grand tome of digital entertainment.

As we peer into the future, speculating on the limitless possibilities, it's essential to remember and honor our past. The 1994-2001 era wasn't just a period of gaming; it was the bedrock upon which our current gaming skyscrapers stand. And as we soar higher, reaching for the digital stars, we must never forget the foundations laid by that gray box and the pioneers of that golden age.

In conclusion, our journey from the past to the present is more than a nostalgia trip. It's a testament to human creativity, innovation, and our innate desire to dream, explore, and connect. As we venture into the brave new worlds of VR, AR, and beyond, we carry with us the lessons, memories, and inspirations of an era that truly set the stage for the wonders of today. The game, dear readers, has only just begun.

# CONCLUSION

## A Final Bow: To Pixels and Passions

In the vast tapestry of memories that constitute our lives, some moments shimmer brighter than others. For me, one of those glinting threads is the soft hum of the PlayStation as it booted up, the unmistakable chime signaling the start of countless adventures. There, on the floor of my childhood bedroom, controller in hand, reality would blur as the world of pixels and polygons beckoned me to explore.

I fondly remember one winter evening, when the snow outside had painted our neighborhood a pristine white. My friends and I huddled together, fingers flying over controllers, as we took turns trying to best each other's scores. The room echoed with laughter, strategy debates, and the occasional friendly jibe. In that moment, it wasn't just about the games. It was about the bond they helped forge, the shared experiences, and the memories we were creating.

Now, having journeyed together through this homage to the 1994-2001 era, it's clear that while technology evolves and platforms change, the essence of gaming remains the same: the joy of discovery, the thrill of challenge, and the camaraderie it brings.

To my parents, who often shook their heads at my gaming marathons but supported my passion nonetheless: thank you.

Your patience and understanding fueled my dreams, even when they seemed as fantastical as the worlds I played in.

To my friends, the co-op partners of my life, who navigated both virtual dungeons and real-life challenges with me: our shared quests, both on-screen and off, have been the stuff of legends. You've been the Tails to my Sonic, the Luigi to my Mario, and for that, I am forever grateful.

Lastly, to the countless developers, artists, musicians, and visionaries who poured their hearts and souls into creating these gaming masterpieces: your dedication has not just entertained, but inspired. You've reminded us of the power of storytelling, the allure of exploration, and the magic of stepping into someone else's shoes, even if just for a little while.

As we stand on the cusp of a new gaming horizon, I'm filled with both nostalgia for the past and excitement for the future. But most of all, I'm grateful. Grateful for the games that shaped my youth, for the people who journeyed alongside me, and for the chance to share this passion with all of you.

Thank you for accompanying me on this pixelated odyssey. Here's to many more adventures, challenges, and shared memories in the vibrant universe of gaming.